Manu V. Devadevan is Assistant Professor of History at the Indian Institute of Technology Mandi, Himachal Pradesh, and author of *A Prehistory of Hinduism* (2016) and *The 'Early Medieval' Origins of India* (2020). A poet, literary critic and translator, he has published widely in Kannada and also writes in Malayalam. Devadevan is a recipient of the Infosys Prize 2019 for Humanities.

God Is Dead, There Is No God

The Vachanas of Allama Prabhu

Translated from the Kannada by

Manu V. Devadevan

SPEAKING TIGER

SPEAKING TIGER BOOKS LLP
4381/4, Ansari Road, Daryaganj
New Delhi 110002

Published in paperback by Speaking Tiger Books 2019

ISBN: 978-93-89692-08-2
eISBN: 978-93-89692-09-9

10 9 8 7 6 5 4 3 2 1

Typeset in Adobe Caslon Pro by SÜRYA, New Delhi
Printed at HT Media Ltd, Gr. Noida

In memory of
M.M. Kalburgi

CONTENTS

PREFACE

It is at once gratifying and humbling to present to the Anglophone reader this translation of the Kannada vachanas of Allama Prabhu, a 12th-century saint-poet, who is widely regarded today as one of the pioneers of Virashaivism. I began work on these translations in December 2012 and abandoned the project in less than a month. I had made considerable progress, with nearly eighty vachanas rendered into English. A.K. Ramanujan's *Speaking of Śiva* and H.S. Shivaprakash's *I Keep Vigil of Rudra*, with their orientation towards formalism and dialectics respectively, were the two existing benchmarks of vachanas in English translation. Insofar as both contained less than 160 vachanas each, I was well past the halfway mark.

The adventure was revived one evening in October 2017 during a conversation with Vinaya Chaitanya, who was with me at my residence in Mandi, Himachal Pradesh, at the time on a month-long visit to share with me a set of his forthcoming translations of religious poetry from Malayalam, and finalize them for publication. Earlier in the day, James Mallinson had come home for lunch, taking time out of his *khechari vidya* (paragliding) tour in Bir. Allama returned to me during the lunch with Jim and Vinaya, and in the evening, when I told Vinaya (who is known for his Malayalam translation of Milarepa and English translation of Akka Mahadevi) of the work I had given up some years ago for no reason as it were, he urged me to get back to it again.

Now that I had taken up the work in all earnest, I realized that the translation was not easy, because of two reasons. Firstly, I had to reckon with the fact that Ramanujan's anthology, which was unsatisfactory for a variety of reasons, happens to be the best-known translation of the vachanas. Hardly representative of the wide-ranging themes and concerns in the surviving corpus, *Speaking of Śiva* had nevertheless attracted a cult following since its publication in 1973. Secondly, the vachanas were contextualized against the backdrop of a history that was doubtless passionately utopian, but was deeply flawed in its assessment of the past. A new English version that could brave Ramanujan's formalist renderings and lock horns with a history that evokes strong passions was a challenge.

These translations have benefitted from encouragement and comments—and at times, both—that I received from Jyotirmaya Sharma, David Shulman, Rahamat Tarikere, K.V. Narayana, Kesavan Veluthat, Sudha Gopalakrishnan, Jesse Ross Knutson, Manorama Tripathy, Shonaleeka Kaul, Gil Ben Herut and Abhilash Malayil, in addition to Vinaya, Jim and Shivaprakash. Suggestions for revision that I received from some of them have been invaluable, although I have not been able to incorporate them in every instance.

I am indebted to Ravi Singh of Speaking Tiger for offering to publish this work, and to my editor, Radhika Shenoy, who shepherded it with great élan.

It was the late M.M. Kalburgi, who advised me to take up the vachanas for translation, for he believed that translation and performance on a stage are the moments when one is closest to the text. And this, he held, assaults us with flashes of understanding that other modes of engagement with a text are incapable of extending. That was in 1998. I didn't give it much thought at the time. A job with the Indian Railway, responsibilities as a trade union activist, and amateur research interests in the rich siddha traditions of northern Karnataka kept me busy. Twenty-one years later, I have the book, but Kalburgi is not here to read it.

INTRODUCTION

Allama Prabhu, the Saint Who Made Sacrilege Worthy of Veneration

This volume introduces the Anglophone reader to the vachanas of Allama Prabhu, a major saint from 12th-century Karnataka. Allama's is a household name in the Kannada-speaking region. He is generally placed in the league of Basava, Akka Mahadevi, Channabasava, Siddharama, and a few other saints, and recognized as one of the founders of Virashaivism. The followers of this sect are now called Lingayats or Virashaivas. Over ten million Lingayats live in Karnataka today, accounting to a sixth of the state's population. Several millions more live in the adjoining states of Kerala, Tamil Nadu, Andhra Pradesh, Telangana, Maharashtra and Goa.

The vachanas were poems composed in the 11th and the 12th century by Shaiva saints, whom tradition identifies as sharanas, protégés of Shiva. Attempts to produce vachanas were made off and on in later times too, and has continued well into our times. The surviving poems are over 20,000 in number, but close to 90 per cent of them are attributed to the 130-odd pioneers of the 11th and the 12th century. Among the pioneers, about half a dozen lived between c. 1050 and 1150 CE. The rest were active in the later half of the 12th century. The Lingayats regard the vachanas as their sacred literature. Within the extant corpus, the poems of Basava, Allama Prabhu and Akka Mahadevi are conferred a pride of place and held in special esteem.*

The 12th century was an age of profound political transformations in the Deccan region. The Kalyana Chalukya state, which exercised overlordship over large parts of central and southern Deccan for close to two centuries, fell apart in the early years of the 1160s, when four of its tributary chiefdoms declared independence and established states of their own: the Seunas in the north, the Kakatiyas in the east, the Hoysalas in the south and the Kalachuris in the west. The Chalukya decline had begun after they faced severe military setbacks at the hands of the Kakatiyas and the Hoysalas. The Hoysala ruler, Narasimha I, put to death one of the last Chalukya kings, Taila III, in a campaign in 1163. Of the four new states, the Kalachuri state was short-lived. Founded in 1162, it had disintegrated by the end of the 1180s. The other three states turned out to be enduring. They collapsed only after repeated attacks from the Delhi Sultanate in the first half of the 14th century.

---

*For a general introduction and sample translation of vachanas, see A.K. Ramanujan, *Speaking of Śiva*, Penguin, New Delhi, 1973; and H.S. Shivaprakash, *I Keep Vigil of Rudra: The Vachanas*, Penguin, New Delhi, 2010.

The disintegration of the Kalyana Chalukyas and the appearance of the four successor states were closely related to the fortunes of the sharanas. Basava and Channabasava lived in the Kalachuri court of king Bijjala II. The Kalachuris and the Seunas both extended Siddharama their patronage. Siddharama remained hostile to the former, but seems to have maintained warm relations with the latter, although he didn't accept their support. Harihara, the first hagiographer of the saints, lived in the Hoysala court of Narasimha I, before moving to Hampi. And in some legends, Palkurike Somanatha, the author of the Telugu *Basavapuranamu*, is said to have found a patron in the Kakatiya ruler, Prataparudra. And as it turns out, all of them—Basava, Channabasava, Siddharama, Harihara, Somanatha—were critical of the political establishments of their times, a sentiment widely shared by most 12th-century sharanas.

Historians regard the work of the sharanas as an ingenious regional expression of the larger South Asian bhakti devotionalism. This assessment, however, is placed within a narrative that is the stuff of romances. The 12th century is represented as one of intense religious ferment, characterized by widespread dissent and protest from a section of the Shaivites against oppressive orthodox beliefs and conventions. We are told that under the leadership of Basava (known with various honorific suffixes as Basavanna, Basavaraja, and Basaveshvara), an enlightened brahman from the town of Bagewadi (now Basavana Bagewadi), the unrest developed into an organized movement against religious bigotry, obscurantism and superstitions, challenging exploitation based on class, caste and gender. Devotees of Shiva from all walks of life, especially from the urban artisan and labouring classes, participated in the movement. They gathered in the city of Kalyana (now Basavakalyana in the Bidar district) in an assembly called the anubhava mantapa (the hall of experience), where they discussed a variety of matters that concerned them, from sublime metaphysics of liberation to the mundane aspects of labour. Basava convened the assembly, another saint, Allama Prabhu, presided over it, and a great number of sharanas—among them Akka Mahadevi, Channabasava, Siddharama, Madivala Machayya and Kinnari Bommayya—participated in it. Their views found expression in the form of vachanas, which they composed in great numbers.

The movement culminated in a revolution in Kalyana. The disregard for caste norms and a pratiloma marriage among the sharanas, involving the daughter of a brahman and the son of a madiga (tanner), caused mayhem. The orthodox sections, and under their influence, the king, persecuted the sharanas. The bride's father, Madhuvayya, and the groom's father, Haralayya, were blinded, and in some accounts, put to death. Enough was enough. One of the sharanas, Jagadeva, who in some versions is accompanied by an aide, Mallibomma, avenged the persecution by murdering the king, Bijjala II. The revolution led to the rise of Virashaivism, a new sect based on principles of equality and egalitarianism. The sect accepted the poems of the torchbearer sharanas as its canon.

Kannada vernacular academia celebrates this event as the Kalyana Revolution (Kalyana Kranti), the Vachana

Movement (Vachana Chaluvali) and the Sharana Movement (Sharana Chaluvali) or the Sharana Uprising (Sharanara Andolana). With a narrative of oppression, revolt, persecution and retribution, capped by a regicide, accounts of the Kalyana Revolution doubtless carry the strong impress of France 1789 and Russia 1917. But as it turns out, the narrative is a fine blend of fact and fiction, drawing extensively upon hagiographic accounts from later times. It has its origins in two sources. The first is the 13th-century Telugu *Basavapuranamu* of Palkurike Somanatha, which gained popularity in Karnataka after the poet Bhima rendered it into Kannada in 1369. In this text, the poet put together hagiographic and anecdotal accounts of a number of Shaiva saints, almost in the form of an anthology. In doing so, he structured the legends in an innovative fashion—whether by design or by innocence, we cannot say—as episodes in a meta-hagiography of Basava. The text became the preeminent source for subsequent reconstructions of Basava's life. The unconnected lives of a number of saints were, in the process, reimagined and placed in a narrative centring on the city of Kalyana. The second source for the narrative is the project begun in the early 15th century by theologians such as Mahalingadeva and Shivaganaprasadi Mahadevayya of compiling the poems of the 12th-century saints. The poems were not unavailable in written forms before the 15th century, but they were in circulation mostly in oral forms. Mahalingadeva, Mahadevayya and their successors brought them together—as well as forged many a poem in the process—in the form of narratives on the life of Allama Prabhu, in which the assembly in Kalyana was the centrepiece as it were. The poems were put into the texts as dialogues between the saints.

Sources from the 12th century point to many an instance of dissent against the orthodoxy, but there is no evidence for large-scale unrest across the region. The story of the assembly in Kalyana is a 13th-century invention. The oldest account on the life of Basava, Harihara's *Basavarajadevara Ragale*, places his activities in the town of Mangalavada in the upper Bhima valley, and not in Kalyana. He is said to have organized regular feeding for the sharanas. There is a passing reference in the *Basavarajadevara Ragale* to his meeting with Allama Prabhu. Akka Mahadevi's meeting with Basava and Allama Prabhu at the anubhava mantapa is not known from any source before the 15th century. And the regicide, which some sources say were carried out at Basava's behest, also had nothing to do with Basava or the sharanas. Epigraphic sources tell us that Jagadeva, who killed Bijjala II, was a henchmen of Someshvara IV, the Chalukya scion who tried to regain control over Kalyana which was at the time held by Bijjala II. Given the frosty relationship that Basava and Bijjala II shared towards the end of their lives, it was not hard for hagiographers to represent the killer, Jagadeva, as a follower of Basava.

It is not possible to maintain the historicity of the existing narrative anymore.* What cannot be called into question,

*On the making of the legend of Kalyana, see Manu V. Devadevan, *A Prehistory of Hinduism*, Warsaw and Berlin, DeGruyter, 2016, chapters 3 and 4.

though, is the revolutionary attitude towards religion that the sharanas brought into effect. Their work changed the religious history of Karnataka in irreversible ways.

Allama Prabhu, a key figure in the narrative, has an enigmatic presence in the religious and literary history of South Asia. No other historical figure in the subcontinent seems to have achieved what he did, viz., leave behind an enviable legacy of intellectual and ascetic influence originating from one of the most cryptic and unintelligible corpuses of poems ever written. His influence in the history of the region can by no means be overstated. Allama was among the three most recognized personalities in the Kannada-speaking region—the other two being Basava and the 16th-century saint-poet, Sarvajna—for several centuries, until the cine actor Raj Kumar surpassed the trio in fame in the 1950s. Outside the Kannada-speaking region, he has been relatively unknown, but familiar to the Natha (Kanphata yogi) tradition as one of the eighty-four siddhas.

Allama's dates are not known, but it is certain that he was active in the fifth and sixth decades of the 12th century. He was born in Balligave, a flourishing town and pilgrim centre in Karnataka. Little is known of his life. From Harihara's *Prabhudevara Ragale*, which is the oldest account that we have of him, we gather that Allama was a drummer in the Goggeshvara temple of Balligave. There, in the temple, he fell in love with a girl who had come for worship, and spent a few years with her, making love. We don't know the girl's name. Harihara calls her the Vine of Desire (Kamalate) and later hagiographers, Illusion (Maya). Like all desires and illusions, this one was also not meant to last. One day, the girl fell ill, and died shortly thereafter. Allama spent many distressful days mourning for her. A chance visit to a temple and a meeting with a saint changed his life. He spent the rest of his days as a renouncer, wandering from place to place, in the course of which he met and had discourses with at least two leading religious leaders of the day, Basava and Siddharama. His journey ended in Srisailam in Andhra.

Much fantastic flesh has been added to this skeletal outline in the course of the making of hagiographic conventions in the following centuries. In the hagiographies, he appears as an epitome of wisdom, a proponent of the theory of void (Shunya), and a great miracle worker. He is made the emperor of the throne of void (shunya simhasana chakravarti) that adorns the anubhava mantapa. Hagiographies also recount his brush with that metaphor for asceticism, Goraksha (Gorakhnath), with whom he is said to have had a debate and a martial combat. The combat makes Allama's system, turning the body into a void (Shunya Kaya), triumph over Goraksha's scheme, making the body hard as diamond (Vajra Kaya).

The hagiographies are important for us to learn how Allama and his works were received in the Kannada-speaking region and also to investigate how institutions and ascetic lineages centring on him were built after the 12th century. Such an exercise is beyond the scope of the humbler objective that this volume has.

Allama composed a large number of poems, how

many, we cannot know for sure. What can be said with certainty is that vachanas spuriously attributed to Allama survive in greater numbers than the genuine ones. The Karnatak University critical edition, *Vyomamuruti Allamaprabhudevara Vachanagalu* (hereafter VAV), on which the present translations are based, contains 1412 poems, along with a vachana on creation, a text called the *Mantragopya*, and twenty-nine songs. L. Basavaraju's edition, *Allamana Vachana Chandrike*, has 1294 vachanas and twenty-seven svara-vachanas (vachanas set to music). The Kannada Pustaka Pradhikara popular edition contains 1636 vachanas, and the popular edition website, www.vachanasanchaya.net, records the number as 1670.*

The vachana is generally held to be a poem in free verse. Ramanujan calls it 'a religious lyric in Kannada free verse'.** In its surviving form, the vachana occurs as free verse for sure. And this resonates well with the propensity among the sharanas to transcend established conventions. There appears to be a grain of truth in the free verse thesis. But this is not indeed the case. The poems were originally composed in metres such as the tripadi, the shatpadi and the ragale.

---

*See *Vyomamuruti Allamaprabhudevara Vachanagalu*, Eds R.C. Hiremath and M.S. Sunkapur, Kannada Adhyayana Peetha, Karnatak University, Dharwad, 1976; *Allamana Vachana Chandrike*, Ed. L. Basavaraju, Lohiya Prakashana, Bellary, 2001 (1960); *Allamaprabhudevara Vachanasamputa*, Ed. B.V. Mallapur, Kannada Pusthaka Pradhikara, Bangalore, 2001 (1993); and vachana.sanchaya.net respectively.

**Ramanujan, *Speaking of Śiva*, p. xi.

These metres, used conventionally for poetry in Kannada, were triplets, hexastiches and couplets respectively, each occurring in a variety of scales. Not all scales were used in the vachanas. The vachanas adhered to another Kannada poetic convention, the second-syllable rhyme, rather scrupulously. Their present form is the result of nearly three centuries of oral circulation, which transformed most of them beyond recognition. But several vestiges of their original form, including the second-syllable rhyme, still remain in them. With some care, it is possible to reconstruct the poems in the metrical form at least in some instances. I will demonstrate this with two poems from the present selection.

Consider poem 9 in the section 'Inhering Within', which begins with the words, 'I saw a flaming Linga in a shrine of wax':

aragina deguladalli ondu uriya lingava kande.
lingava poojisuva goravanadettalada hodano?
uttarapathada darshanadigalige
suttimuttida maye ettalike hoyittu.
maranolagana kichchu marana suttada kande.
goggeshvaralingavadettalada hodano?

This is a free verse. We propose to make two major changes in them, viz., repeat the word gorava found in the second line again in the last line, and read darshana in the third line as tatvashastra, without a serious change in meaning, as these are required for the second-syllable rhyme scheme. Other changes are only of syntax and readjustment of vocabulary for metrical purposes. The result is a tripadi poem in the Kusuma metre, which is in the form of combinations with a maximum of ten short and a minimum of four long syllables and two short syllables in the first two lines, and a maximum of sixteen short and a minimum of six long syllables and four short syllables in the third line.

aragu deguladalli
uriya lingava kande,
gorava poojusadettaladutihano?

uttarapathadalli
tatvashastragalannu
suttimuttida maye ettalihudo?

maranoladagida kichchu
marana suttada kande,
gorava goggeshvaranoladutihano?

The second example is poem 2 in the section 'Passions of the Void', 'the void sowed the void'.

bayalu bayalane bitti
bayalu bayalane beledu
bayalu bayalagi bayalayittayya.

bayala jeevana,
bayala bhavane,
bayalu bayalagi bayalayittayya.

nimma poojisidavaru
munnave bayaladaru,
na nimma nambi bayalade goggeshvara.

There is very little to be done here to make it a tripadi in the Kusuma metre. The fourth and the fifth lines, bayala jeevana 'void's life' and bayala bhavane 'void's imagination', are both incomplete in terms of meaning. Adding the word bayalu, 'void', at both places will make them complete as well as fit them into the metre. The last three lines call for three minor changes in vocabulary: i) replace nimma, 'you' in the honorific plural with ninna, 'you' in the singular ii) remove the emphasis ve from munnave, and change the past perfect, bayaladaru, to the past perfect continuous, bayalagiharu and iii) change na nimma nambi, 'with faith in you' to ninnalli, 'in you'. We then have a metrically perfect poem with the second-syllable rhyming:

bayalu bayalane bitti
bayalu bayalane beledu
bayalu bayalagi bayalayittayya.

bayala jeevana bayalu,
bayala bhavane bayalu,
bayalu bayalagi bayalayittayya

ninna poojisidavaru
munna bayalagiharu,
ninnalli bayalade goggeshvara.

A good number of poems can be metrically restored, but most of them have transformed extensively with only the rhyming second syllable occurring as clue that they were actually metrical compositions.

'Goggeshvara', the name of the deity that Allama had worshipped in Balligave as a drummer, figures in all his poems as the signature. The word changed into several other forms in the course of its oral transmission, and occurs in the manuscripts in at least six variants in addition to Goggeshvara, viz., Gogeshvara, Goheshvara, Guheshvara, Guhyeshvara, Gumheshvara and Gopeshvara. The third one of these, Guheshvara, is the most popular, which may have to do with its association with the cavern (guhe, from Sanskrit guha) and the picture of mysteries that it brings to mind. There has been considerable intellectual kite-flying in our times to unpack 'the mysterious' in the cavern that Allama is thought to be invoking. In his translation, Ramanujan renders the signature as 'Lord of Caves'* and attempts a fanciful explanation as well.**

As a temple drummer, Allama was a devotee of Shiva. After renunciation, he began to free himself from this status of submission and set out to explore what the entity that goes by the name of Goggeshvara (or Shiva) is and how it could be understood. This concern produced several points of intersection as well as major divergences with the poems of his contemporaries. We must therefore place his poems in

---

*Ramanujan, *Speaking of Śiva*, pp. 131-150.

**Ibid., p. 126.

the new religious and intellectual climate that the sharanas had begun to generate.

The sharanas upheld a set of ideals that had gained ground by the mid-12th century. The first of these was opposition to the temple. In a famous poem of Basava, we hear:

> The rich make temple for Shiva.
> What'll I make, My Lord,
> Poor that I'm?
>
> My legs are pillars indeed,
> My body, the shrine,
> My head, My Lord, is the golden pinnacle.
>
> Listen, Koodalasangamadeva,
> The standing will cease to be,
> The moving will not.*

Allama expressed a similar sentiment when in one of his poems he said:

> Goggeshvara,
> I saw the shrine flee
> When the Lord arrived.

(Relationship; 2)

**Basavannavara Vachanagalu*, Ed. L. Basavaraju, Sapna Book House, Bangalore, 2017 (1952), No. 448.

The more prominent among the sharanas—Allama, Basava, Siddharama, Akka Mahadevi, Madivala Machayya—were associated with temples in some capacity or the other. Opposition to temple worship seems to have had its roots in the prohibition on temple entry for untouchable castes. In the 11th century, Devara Dasimayya, a pioneering sharana and a weaver by profession, had made an implicit attack on the idea of temple worship, because pooja in a temple was performed by a mediating entity, the priest, and not by the devotee. Said Dasimayya:

> Making love with the wife,
> Offering the grand feast,
> Worshipping the lord of the world—
>
> Will they have these done by others
> When they are sane,
> Ramanatha?*

The second ideal was the rejection of pilgrimage. It is neither uncommon today for Lingayats to go on pilgrimage, nor hard to find sharanas travelling to pilgrim centres like Srisailam in the hagiographies. But the sharanas developed an attitude of reticence towards pilgrimage. There was, Basava held, only one land for a scavenger's street and a shrine of Shiva to stand.** In one of her poems, Akka Mahadevi says:

**Devara Dasimayyana Vachanagalu*, Ed. L. Basavaraju, Geetha Book House, Mysore, 2012 (1970), No. 33.

***Basavannavara Vachanagalu*, No. 474.

Is it false
        That the courtyard
        Of a devotee of Shiva
        Is Varanasi?

There are sixty-eight pilgrim centres
        In the courtyard of a devotee of Shiva.

Srisaila as one moves around,
Kedara at the corners,
Out from there, the sacred Varanasi.

Detachment was the seed,
        Devotion the sprout!

Channamallikarjuna, My Lord,
        The courtyard of your devotee
        Is greater than Varanasi, look!*

A third ideal was the disregard for kinship and inherited relationships. 'Devotion to kinship is supreme hell,' Basava declared.** Its corollary was the disregard for caste-based identities. Here is Basava's take on it:

Will I call Siriyala a merchant?
I call Machayya a washer man?

**Akkana Vachanagalu*, Ed. L. Basavaraju, Geetha Book House, Mysore, 2012 (1966), No. 173.

***Basavannavara Vachanagalu*, No. 397.

Call Kakkayya a leather dyer?
Channayya a tanner?

Koodalasangama will laugh at me,
Should I say I'm a brahman, My Friend.*

Basava's poems have a distinct quality that few other sharanas share. As a brahman who had cast away his thread of investiture and rejected the caste system, there is an element of missionary zeal in his work for bringing the sacred to the less fortunate devotees of Shiva. This was an impossible objective from within the orthodox order of things. The way out involved a rejection of the existing hierarchies, beliefs and forms of worship and putting in place a new order of things. In doing so, Basava was replacing the metaphysical with the ethical. It involved an approach of compassion towards the self and making the individual charged with volition, freedom and sacredness. This is the implication of visualizing the body as a temple and the substance behind the declaration, 'the standing will cease to be, the moving will not'.

Allama's approach to the orthodoxy of his times did not differ from Basava's, but his project was a move in the other direction. He replaced the ethical with the metaphysical, a line of thinking that involved the erasure of ethics as a category. Allama was aware that the self and the system are products of ethics, and that these were the sources

*Ibid., No. 217.

of worldly attachments and bondages in which the woes of humankind have their origin. The need, then, was to decenter the self and the system, and place the phenomenal world on a metaphysical plane. Here is a poem that rejects the self:

Did I say sound?
  The spittle of the ear!
Did I say touch?
  The spittle of the skin!
Did I say form?
  The spittle of the eye!
Did I say taste?
  The spittle of the tongue!
Did I say fragrance?
  The spittle of the nose!
Did I say I?
  The spittle of learning!

Goggeshvara-linga
  Is the light of the dawn
  When the ruin called 'spittle'
  Has come to pass.

(Knowing, Remembering and Forgetting; 8)

And here's one that is critical of systems:

The Vedas went astray,
  As they failed to breach.

The sciences went astray,
As they failed to accomplish.
The lore went astray,
As they failed to fulfill.
The elders went astray,
As they failed to know themselves.

Their intellect devoured them.

Do they know you,
Goggeshvara?

(Knowing, Remembering
and Forgetting; 3)

In this line of reasoning, Allama's treatment of the body becoming a temple had to differ from Basava's and take a different orientation. As a devotee of Goggeshvara in his younger days, he is likely to have regarded the body as a shrine.

Why another shrine
When there's one in the body?

No one asked for two,
My Lord.

Goggeshvara,
What am I,
When you're a stone?

(The Body; 3)

This does not stop him from wondering if the body is resourceful enough to keep the deity installed within.

The legs became the pillar,
My Lord,
My body turned into a shrine.

My tongue, the bell,
My head, the golden pinnacle,
What's up, My Lord?

My breath was the Linga's throne,
My Lord.

Goggeshvara,
I stayed in a way
That didn't topple
Your Pranalinga,
Installed in me.

(The Body; 2)

He has to finally contend that

The deity called life
Finding worship
In the body, the shrine
At the hands of the senses, the priests

Is faraway
From Goggeshvara-linga.

(Devotion and Worship; 13)

His quest for the nature of Goggeshvara might have begun with devotion and submission to the lord, but it led him in the end to the realization that the lord, as an entity outside of us, does not exist. There are several poems that capture this awareness. Here are two of them:

> In the abode where nothing exists,
> The self created
> 'You' and 'I'.
> What if a thousand things are told
> Of what 'doesn't exist'
> And 'does exist'?
>
> If 'does exist'
> Can be made 'doesn't exist',
> Isn't 'doesn't exist'
> Goggeshvara?
>
> (The Word; 9)

> Not on earth,
> Not in the sky.
> Neither in the fourteen world of worlds,
> Nor yonder.
> I don't know what happened,
> My dear.
>
> Goggeshvara wasn't then,
> Isn't now,
> And never will be.
>
> (God Is Dead, There's No God; 11)

Where, then, does the lord dwell? Allama contends that Goggeshvara is a product of a devotee's mind and does not have an existence outside of it.

'Smaller than a grain
    And greater than the great',
These words are false!

Is there deluge
    Where the Linga stands?

Goggeshvara is nowhere
    Other than in the devotees'
    Acts of the mind.

(The Word; 7)

This is a major departure from the position he might have held earlier that the lord is a reality that remains concealed. This older view finds expression in the poem below:

Your bond with the protégé is

    Like fire in the stone,
    Like reflection in the water,
    Like tree in the seed,
    Like silence in the sound,

Goggeshvara.

(Shiva's Protégés; 1)

Here is another poem that gives the same sense:

Your ways are
Like the treasure
Shielded under the earth,
Like the lightning
Shielded in the cloud,
Like the mirage
Shielded in the field,
Like the light
Shielded behind the eyes,

Goggeshvara.

(Relationships; 6)

We confront an Allama who begins by acknowledging the phenomenal reality of the lord, but arrives at the realization that 'Goggeshvara wasn't then, isn't now, and will never be.' The reality is a void, shunya or bayalu.

That I've known
Is void indeed.
That I haven't
Is void indeed.

Goggeshvara is void indeed
In knowing,
Sign,
And forgetting.

(Passions of the Void; 4)

At some levels, Allama's representation of Goggeshvara as a void has close parallels to the understanding of void that Nagarjuna had developed in his *Mulamadhyamakakarika* and the *Vigrahavyavartani*. In a poem that bears this out, he says:

There's neither truth,
    Nor untruth.
Neither born together,
    Nor not born together.

Neither I,
    Nor you.
Neither 'Neither!'
    Nor 'Nor!'

What's called Goggeshvara
    Is a void indeed.

(Passions of the Void; 9)

The void that Allama speaks of is not a static state of existence, but a force imbued with the power to create and transform. It must be realized, though, that what it creates and transforms is void itself.

The void sowed the void,
    The void raised the void,
    The void turned into void
    To become the void.

The void's life is void,
The void's acts of the mind, void,
The void turned into void
To become the void.

They that worshipped you
Became the void long ago.

I worshipped you
To become the void,
Goggeshvara.

(Passions of the Void; 2)

This dynamic void is the source of everything, including Goggeshvara.

In the void where nothing exists,
There arose a colour
Born of thought.

The void assumed a form
When it embellished the colour.

Isn't the beauty of such a form
The first frame of
Our Goggeshvara-linga?

(Passions of the Void; 13)

Allama's void is a potent force. It cannot for that reason be compared with the nothingness of Sartre and Heidegger or with the absence of essential attributes (svabhava) that Nagarjuna identifies as shunya. The void here is also not ontological. It is primarily an aspect of cognition. It represents the dynamism of the mind in a tabula rasa state, with freedom to interpret without the mediation of convention or of an agency from outside. And the interpretation happens through imageries and not through words. See, for instance, Allama's approach to the word in this poem:

Who offered butter
    And gave a name
    To the child called
    Formlessness?
Ho! Ho! Ho!
    Look at the diffidence of the word!

(The Word; 5)

and in this:

Can the metal bruise the body
    After it melts into a mass?

Sangana Basavanna,
How can those that speak
    In the non-duality of words
    Know Goggeshvara-linga?

(The Word; 2)

and here:

It didn't touch in the three,
It didn't show in the six,
It wasn't found in the eight,
It didn't stand in the one.

What do I tell of it?
How do I describe it?

It didn't decline in the body.
It didn't remain in the breath.

The Linga called Goggeshvara
Didn't appear in the word.

(The Word; 3)

Interpretation through imageries has the power to produce awareness without reducing it to meaning, and can in this sense upset established meanings through symbolic reversals and recantations. The awareness through imageries that springs from void is devoid of meaning, like the dream of an infant.

The crop without the earth is
The royal meal,
The nameless food.

The cow, untouched by the bull—

I found the butter, and ate it up,
When there was none to churn.

Goggeshvara is the nameless void,
Like an infant's dream.

(Passions of the Void; 18)

For in Allama's understanding, isn't Goggeshvara the passion of the void, rather than its essence or meaning?

The seed of the sky
Was made of fire.
It sprouted and grew
With no branches.
It destroyed him that said
He knew.

O Man, unaware of this judgement,

Goggeshvara is
The passion of the void.

(Passions of the Void; 12)

The scheme of void rejects all aspects of representation that produces meaning. And these include narratives, which in Allama's times had a robust presence across India in their kavya and itihasa-purana guises. Allama repudiates narratives with the force of sacrilege. Look at these words:

Goddess Ganga
　　Became a tonsured widow.

Goddess Gauri
　　Lost her earrings.

The moon and the sun
　　Bathed for pollution.

The Wind God
　　Bore the carriage heavenward-bound.

Vasudeva
　　Ripped the skull apart.

News from there:
　　Goggeshvara is dead!
　　　　(God Is Dead, There's No God; 4)

Or these words:

The horns of Aja—
　　The creator of the world—
　　Broke.
The sun and the moon on earth
　　Fell on the ground.

It's sunset
　　When the sunrise has stopped.

The village was scorched,
The sound ended.

What wonder is this?

The God perished,
The Goddess went whoring,
I prevailed,
Goggeshvara. (God Is Dead, There's No God; 2)

Or these, for that matter:

Ah, the elders,
Great and matching warriors of renown,
Have lost their mind
And driven mad!

The God perished,
Brahma carried,
Vishnu held the fire.
Ganga and Gauri
Became tonsured widows.

I saw this in alarm,
Goggeshvara.
(God Is Dead, There's No God; 3)

These words would be more than sacrilege today. It is not hard to guess what would have become of Allama for uttering these words, had he lived in our times. He would have met the very fate that met the old man to whom we have dedicated this book.

The long and short of this discussion is that Allama's thought was anti-systemic to the last letter, so much so that it perfected a metaphysics that had room only for awareness as an immanent experiential reality. It closed its doors on the self, on meaning, on an ontologically constituted world, and on the ultimate godhead, Shiva in his form as Goggeshvara. This was at once a rather brazen way of showing Shiva his place and an ingenious way of undermining the world of power structures, hierarchies, conventions and rituals. It was also an experiment with freedom taken to its proverbial extreme, freedom from liberation and the dreams, visions and promises it precipitates.

Allama is now regarded as one of the greatest yogis of all times, and his indecipherably cryptic poems seen as symbolic or coded representations of his yogic experience. These are not fully modern views. They have persisted since the 15th century, when attempts were made to domesticate Allama's vachanas through exegesis produced on them, and his obscure imageries interpreted as signifying ideas and aspects of ascetic practices. The exegesis related them to a set of familiar staples that had their origins in various schools of asceticism, including yoga, sankhya and the multiple systems of vedanta. We must be sorry for what he is reduced to, for the new void-based metaphysics that

Allama constructed struck at the heart of ideas such as yoga, yogic experience and liberation.

We must then conclude that Allama's presence in Karnataka as one of the most influential figures in her history was the outcome of a failure, a failure on the part of post 12th-century Karnataka to understand the character of Allama's enterprise, and conversely, a failure on Allama's part to appreciate the ethical and phenomenal powers of his void-based metaphysics. After all, void was a powerful idea; an image and a signifier potent enough to create systems, exegesis and a hermeneutics of its own that had the force to abuse its original principles into incapacity and drive them out of existence. It could, in this sense, simply become what it had in the first place repudiated. And that is what it precisely became. Allama's metaphysics was integrated into the system that Virashaivism began to develop from the early 15th century onwards. The rest is a travesty of his life and works. We call it history.

THE MIST OF MAYA

1.

I found the abode
        Where the five great sins go.
The abode
        Where all sorrows swelter.
I found the abode
        Where death is kicked with the feet.
The abode
        Where Kama's hands are cut off.
I found the abode
        Where Maya's mouth is crushed.

With my eyes full,
        I found Goggeshvara-linga
        On my palmtop.

(VAV 768)

2.

The scourge of Maya
Took the ones born of separation.

They didn't know
That formlessness is its form.

Goggeshvara,
Look at the trouble of calling it
With a name.

(VAV 311)

3.

The forest is target,
When wildfire erupts,

The sea, target,
When water-fire erupts,

The body, target,
When body-fire erupts,

The world, target,
When the fire of death erupts.

The abusers are target,
When the fire of rage erupts
In the minds of Shiva's protégés.

Listen,
I'm no target
To the furious fire of your Maya,
Goggeshvara.

(VAV 1063)

4.

The hunting sport that the Three-Eyed played
Casting the net of
Brahma, the rope
And Vishnu, the Maya,
And displaying gold, woman, and land—

You slew it with no disgust,
Hurling
The mouthful called desire,
Ah! Goggeshvara.

(VAV 21)

5.

Look how it learnt that
I'm a fool
Caught in Maya's web.

Look how it learnt that
It's the Linga.

Look how the self
Came to its own delight
And learnt that
It's Goggeshvara
Beyond thought and form.

(VAV 11)

6.

Tell me, who made this feeling
    Of 'You' and 'I'?

'You' is ignorance,
    'I', a captive to Maya.

When the bliss
    Of what's not 'You' or 'I'
    Is known without difference,

    The delight is offered you,
    Goggeshvara.

(VAV 562)

7.

When the mist of Maya
Infuses the mango tree,
        Why do the flower,
        Bud, and fruits
        Not fall off?

Look, Goggeshvara,
        I'll not touch the fruit
        When it grows in abundance.

(VAV 346)

8.

I saw a Maya on the roadway.
It showed the way to another place,
  It showed the way to another place.

  'There!'
  'There!'
  'There!'

Goggeshvara's scribes
  Are vile indeed.

(VAV 239)

9.

Gold is Maya, they say,
Woman is Maya, they say,
The earth is Maya, they say.

Gold is not Maya,
Woman is not Maya,
The earth is not Maya.

Look, Goggeshvara,
The desire before the mind
Is Maya indeed.

(VAV 72)

10.

Does knowing come for a naught,
When the filth of Maya
        Hasn't left the mind,
When the body's distress
        Hasn't left the trace?

Can the self be realized for a naught,
        Dear fool!

Learn for yourself what you're,
        If you can know
        Goggeshvara-linga.

(VAV 373)

11.

All words are wisdom
When the self knows the self,
Look!

All words are Maya
When the self forgets the self,
Look!

Are words of a Shivayogi
That forgets after knowing
Anything more than instructions?

When I speak to clear
The worries in your mind,
There's no stain in my mind,
Look!

I opened my mouth only because
You're the child of
Our Goggeshvara-linga's compassion.

Tell me, dear fool,
Why else have I?

(VAV 1276)

12.

When Maya was given the palm leaf and stylus,
    She wrote the good and bad omens,
    Look.
When the image of wax was draped
    In a garment of fire,
    It turned into the rich finery,
    Look.

The parrot sporting in the sky
Devoured the cat in the cage
    And moved away
    From Rambha's shoulders,*
    Look, Goggeshvara.

(VAV 36)

---

*Rambha is a nymph (apsara) in Indra's service.

BIRTH AND DEATH

1.

The time of death is sixty—
        Death knows death itself.
The time of death is fifty—
        Death knows death itself.
The time of death is forty—
        Death knows death itself.
The time of death is thirty—
        Death knows death itself.
The time of death is twenty—
        Death knows death itself.
The time of death is ten—
        Death knows death itself.

Channabasavanna,
        If you know the death of these deaths,
        Make it known in Goggeshvara-linga.

(VAV 1249)

2.

Of all transformations,
The transformation of the mind
Is delightful.

Of all unions,
The union of the protégés
Is delightful.

Fools, born with bodies,
Learning the secret of not dying
Is indeed delightful,
Goggeshvara.

(VAV 538)

3.

There're three wells
On the body's ground.

He that touched the first well
Became the body's companion.
He that touched the well in between
Was thrown to birth, existence, and death.
He that touched the upper well
Found release within his lifetime.

Look, the protégés,
Given to Goggeshvara-linga,
Went without stroking or touching them,
To transcend the supreme brahma!

(VAV 618)

4.

Will I ask all those born
        Not to be born?
Will I ask all those having
        Not to have?
Will I ask all those who perish in the deluge
        Not to perish?

Goggeshvara,
        After knowing you,
        And merging in you,
        Will I ask those on earth
        Not to live?

(VAV 436)

5.

Child with no parents,
    Haven't you taken birth
    And grown up on your own?

Weren't you fulfilled in the breath
    With your transformation?

Weren't you sparkling on your own,
    Incapable of being divided
    By those who divide?

Goggeshvara,
    Your trait is inherent in you.

(VAV 765)

6.

Leaping into the flaming fire

One shouldn't think
It swelters;

One shouldn't think
It doesn't swelter.

Look Goggeshvara,
There's no birth again
When held and scorched,
And the ashes smeared.

(VAV 603)

7.

Ah!
You refused to remain unknowing
        And ended up as a sign
        By knowing!

Have the elders assembled,
        Master,
        And yoked you
        To their sacraments?

Ah!
        You've ended up
        As a companion to death,
        Goggeshvara!

(VAV 517)

8.

The city of the beginning,
        The city of the Vedas,
The city of snows,
        The divided,
        The undivided—

Ho! Ho! Ho!
        The mind devoured the motion!

Goggeshvara,
        The beginning devoured the Veda,
        The Veda devoured the self-born,

        Your protégés
        Were released
        From death and fate.

(VAV 452)

9.

What talk is this
Of merging in the Linga
After death?

Look,
It's false!

Look, Siddharamayya,
The protégés that have known Goggeshvara-linga
Will be pleased
If the self is known before death
And exists as itself.

(VAV 806)

10.

O Man with a body—
Instant born
And dying in no time—

Tell me,
When will you be known as god?

Tell me,
What's the difference between god
And the dying,
Were god to die?

The divine world is
For the gods,

The human world
For humans.

There's no other world
For Goggeshvarallayya.

(VAV 503)

11.

The footless teacher
Has a headless disciple.

The sacrilegious teacher
Has a disciple failing the vow.

Goggeshvara,
In you I seek
The death
The teacher and the disciple died.

(VAV 630)

12.

The creatures born at the hour of sunrise
Have gone in the sunset, Ho!
Beings with bodies, living by the day,
Have gone on the road they came, Ho!

The Linga called Goggeshvara
Is for no one, my friend!

(VAV 983)

KNOWING, REMEMBERING AND FORGETTING

1.

I saw in a dream
The elephant from the sky,
Huge as the world.

What shall I speak of it,
My dear!
How shall I speak of the great might,
My dear!

Forgetting the Linga called Goggeshvara
After knowing it
Is like a carriage
Running on the aloe plant.

(VAV 677)

2.

I don't know
How many deluges have gone.
I don't know
How many deluges are to come.

Deluge is when
One's own state isn't known.
Deluge is when
Words turn against oneself.

Goggeshvara,
Are there
Such deluges in you?

(VAV 655)

3.

The Vedas went astray,
        As they failed to breach.
The sciences went astray,
        As they failed to accomplish.
The lore went astray,
        As they failed to fulfill.
The elders went astray,
        As they failed to know themselves.

Their intellect devoured them.

Do they know you,
        Goggeshvara?

(VAV 324)

4.

'We've known,'
'We've known,' you say.

Tell me,
What've you known?

Do they say, 'we've known',
If they've indeed known?

Goggeshvara,
Those who've known
The unknowable might
Exist as if they haven't.

(VAV 362)

5.

What knowing is it
        That knows the self?

What forgetting is it
        That forgets the self?

Look, Goggeshvara,
        They that know and forget
        Exist like your image.

(VAV 372)

6.

I was listening to the quarters
One after the other,
Like the bird on the speaking tree.

Nobody that knows!
Nobody that knows!

Known and vanished,
My friend!

Goggeshvara remained
Himself in himself
Like a hailstone
That fell into the lake.

(VAV 666)

7.

Can you look
For the shaft of wax
After shooting it
At the cinder hill?

Does the shrine of Shiva,
Made of snow,
Have a capstone
Of sunlight?

Can there be
Remembering again,
After the linga
Called Goggeshvara is known?

(VAV 1263)

8.

Did I say sound?
        The spittle of the ear!
Did I say touch?
        The spittle of the skin!
Did I say form?
        The spittle of the eye!
Did I say taste?
        The spittle of the tongue!
Did I say fragrance?
        The spittle of the nose!
Did I say I?
        The spittle of learning!

Goggeshvara-linga
        Is the light of the dawn
        When the ruin called 'spittle'
        Has come to pass.

(VAV 564)

9.

Tell me,
What were you
Before I had known myself?

I found through your eyes that
You had kept your mouth shut.

When you opened your mouth to speak
After I had known myself,
I looked at it bashfully
With my eyes,
Look!

You who looks at me,
And I, who look at you
Have the same stealthy gaze,
Look!

Goggeshvara,
I learnt the cleverness of your secret,
Look!

(VAV 10)

10.

What's this darkness
Before the eyes?

What's this forgetfulness
Before the mind?

A battleground within,
Lovemaking without!

What's this beaten track,
Goggeshvara?

(VAV 316)

11.

That I've seen
Is the forgetting of the eyes.
That I haven't
Is the forgetting of the mind.
That I united
Is the forgetting of memory.
That I departed
Is the forgetting of forgetting.

Listen, Mother-dear,

When the polluting madness
Of seeing,
Not seeing,
Uniting
And departing
Are expelled,

It's impossible
To depart from Goggeshvara-linga.

(VAV 1273)

12.

No!
The sight has no sight
        In front of it.

What if it's made?
        What if it isn't?

No!
The sign of the knowledge
Called Goggeshvara
        Isn't in front.

What if it's made?
        What if it isn't?

(VAV 636)

13.

The loud became
　　A simile for the tree
The silent,
　　A simile for the stone.
The angry,
　　A simile for fire,
The restful,
　　A simile for water.
The one who says 'I know' became
　　A simile for absence,
The one who says 'I don't know' became
　　A simile for a beast.

For this reason
Not one do I see
That became a simile
　　For the Linga called Goggeshvara,
　　Without saying
　　'I know',
　　Or 'I don't',
　　And remained after wiping out
　　The sign of knowing.

(VAV 491)

14.

The spotless sages
Who've won the self—

Can they be looked upon like the rest,
    As they speak like the rest,
    Behave like the rest,
    And embrace the world
    Like the rest?

Can the seed of knowing Shiva—
Shining bright at the core of their mind—
    Be hollow?

Goggeshvara,
    Can a worm take the fire
    Even when it's not ablaze?

(VAV 1267)

THE WAYS OF THE WORLD

1.

The mouse
Rushing across the attic
Gave a slip to the cat in wait
And hid in its eye.

The eye and the mouse together
Did not see
Goggeshvara-linga.

(VAV 1214)

2.

They found the form,
    Not the formless.
They found fitness,
    Not the body.
They found the acts,
    Not the thoughts.

Goggeshvara,
    They found your sign,
    But went astray,
    As they failed to merge.

(VAV 495)

3.

Look at the fight of the dogs
Come to dine,
When the corpse called the world
Has fallen,
My friends!

The corpse rises
To laugh at the fighting dogs.

Look,
The linga called Goggeshvara
Isn't there,
My friends.

(VAV 46)

4.

A billion perished for desire,
A billion perished for flesh.
A billion perished for gold,
        Woman,
        And land.

Goggeshvara,
        Not one do I see
        That perished for you.

(VAV 91)

5.

There's no cause,
No effect.
Why do you say
You've become devotees?

You dine
On the spittle of the five mouths.
You know the face
Of the five women.
You don't know how to
Free the three shackles.

Goggeshvara,
Look at their delusion that
They've grabbed the body
To touch the Linga.

(VAV 116)

6.

Won't the tiger devour
When they rush to the forest
For fear of thieves?

Won't the serpent devour
When they rush to the anthill
For fear of the tiger?

Won't karma devour
When they become devotees
For fear of death?

Goggeshvara,
What shall I tell
Of the folks in false costumes
Falling prey to death?

(VAV 73)

7.

They wash the outer and drink,
As they know not
How to wash the inner,
My Lord.

Unable to know
The water that washed the feet
Or the offering,

They drown
In the beaten track,
Goggeshvara.

(VAV 161)

8.

It's come to be
A Linga for me,
A Linga for you,
A Linga for home.

Devotion is washed away,
With the waters,
Ah!

Goggeshvara,
Can the mind touch the Linga
Untouched by the chisel.

(VAV 207)

9.

Why long for a bed
        For making love?

Does the craving fool
        Know disgrace?

Why the desire and worry of worship
        For the protégé that has known you?

Why a touchstone
        For gold, pure as gold?

Does Goggeshvara-linga
        Have a sign?

(VAV 425)

10.

Wearing the garb of the doll made of water,
Wrapped in the fire-hued blanket,
Whirling along in the speed of wind—

    What do these creatures know of god,
    Goggeshvara?

(VAV 721)

DEVOTION AND WORSHIP

1.

The pinnaclеd shrine of Shiva
Has two square pillars
And three traits.

Who're the priests?
Who're those communing, now?
Who're going to worship, now?

Goggeshvara,
Who knows the state and fate
Of its abode?

(VAV 194)

2.

When the static of
The bhuva* world
Was showered in the waters of
The satya** world
And worshipped with flowers from
The deva world,
Sacraments of the ten worlds
Went astray.
Kings of the three worlds
Turned naïve.

Goggeshvara-linga became
Static to the static!

(VAV 197)

---

*The second of the seven worlds in the cosmology of the Vedas.

**The last of the seven worlds in the cosmology of the Vedas.

3.

Five serpents
Have a single body
And two fangs.

I saw the corpse
That died of snakebite,
Whirling!

Goggeshvara,
Where is devotion
In the abode
That doesn't know this eternal.

(VAV 74)

4.

The face of the heart turned dark
When they went to worship
At the face of sunrise.

Pranalinga flew away.
The sanctum fell,
Shattered.

Goggeshvara,
Look at the agony
Of the kinsmen
Who yoke and let go!

(VAV 216)

5.

Don't spend time
Worshipping the bead.

Don't spend time
Worshipping the stone.

The thought of the self will do,
Even if it's for
A fleeting moment.

The thought of the self will do,
Even if it's for
Half a fleeting moment.

Goggeshvara,
Does water have
The trait of fire
Called heat?

(VAV 1011)

6.

Devotion is when it's done
        Before seeking.

Do the Linga and Jangama seek?

For the one that seeks
And the one that's sought,
        There's no offering,
        Goggeshvara.

(VAV 157)

7.

They don't know
        What the five great sins are.

Making a devotee of the worldly
        Is the first sin.
Seeking refuge in the devotee
        Is the second sin.
The teacher
        Is the third sin.
Accepting offerings from the teacher,
        The Linga,
        And the wandering saint,
        Is the fourth sin.
Rendering great devotion
        To Goggeshvara-linga,
        Is the fifth sin.

(VAV 552)

8.

Hey you, with the formless form!
You, of reverse character!
Lingayya!
Is it proper to be worshipped
        By those destined to die?

Look, Goggeshvara,
        It's shameful to be
        Worshipped by those
        Destined to die or endure pain.

(VAV 498)

9.

The sky is the pot,
    Space the water.
The sun and the moon are both flowers,
    Look!

Brahma is the fume,
Vishnu, the lamp,
Rudra, the food.

It's the offering,
    Look!

It's the worship of
    Goggeshvara-linga,
    Look!

(VAV 415)

10.

When the hill catches cold,
	What'll they cover it with,
	Master?

When the void goes naked,
	What'll they clothe it with,
	Master?

When the devotee becomes worldly,
	What'll I compare it with,
	Goggeshvara?

(VAV 109)

11.

A lake on the sky.

They all wash their face
And gather flowers in the water.

No escape from the supreme hell
When they wash the God's face,
Offer worship,
And pray.

Goggeshvara,
What shall I tell
Of the reticence
Of the goblins in heaven!

(VAV 422)

12.

We can sketch
The shape of the great picture,
But can we sketch the breath,
My Lord?

We can have lessons in the acts
Told in the sacred books,
But can we've devotion,
My Lord?

You're the one
Pervading
In the devotion called breath.

Goggeshvara,
You're where this trait is.
You aren't, where it isn't.

(VAV 79)

13.

The deity called life
Finding worship
In the body, the shrine
At the hands of the senses, the priests

Is faraway
From Goggeshvara-linga.

(VAV 1050)

14.

The fire god,
        The cinder god,
The fierce god,
        The burning ground god—

        They're gossiping:
        He's a roving beggar.

I worshipped you,
        Became a lost child,
        Fell on the forlorn road,

        And was ruined,
        Goggeshvara.

(VAV 545)

SHIVA'S PROTÉGÉS

1.

Your bond with the protégé is

Like fire in the stone,
Like reflection in the water,
Like tree in the seed,
Like silence in the sound,

Goggeshvara.

(VAV 1)

2.

The devotee is a pollutant.

He that's merged with the Linga
Fails the vow.

He that says,
'The protégé is the wife, linga the husband
Is an all-virtuous and beneficial word'
Is a reveller incapable of enjoying
The sense organs.

Goggeshvara,
Your protégé
Isn't given to fear,
Nor lost in the acts.

(VAV 523)

3.

The protégés born in awareness,
His forgetting spent—

Can his ways be known?
Can his movement be known?

Goggeshvara,
Your protégés exist
Like a child's dream.

(VAV 384)

4.

A plant grew on the land
Where the ground doesn't stand.

It had eight flowers
Of the lightning colour,
Look!

The fruit appeared on the branch
And ripened in the root.

Goggeshvara,
He is no protégé,
Without eating the fruit
That fell on the spot
That none have ever seen.

(VAV 532)

5.

A sky-coloured whore
    In the fire's body.
The whore has five children,
    Look!

What wonder is this
    When the three worlds stand
    In alarm,
    Going mad at the children's
    Hands and mouth?

Goggeshvara,
    Not one can attain
    The supreme core of the self
    Other than the protégé,
    Who'll sketch the dark-coloured fog
    And make love.

(VAV 322)

6.

The weight of the eye
Is heavy on the Linga.

Does the protégé speak
To beings embodied?

Goggeshvara,
Your protégé
Is innocent
In deed and word.

(VAV 364)

7.

Limbs all over the body
For the river that flows.

Tongue all over the body
For the fire that blazes.

Face all over the body
For the wind that blows.

Goggeshvara,
Your protégé
Has Linga
For all his organs.

(VAV 1265)

8.

When the humans of the mortal world
Made a god in the temple,
I was alarmed, My Lord.

I was alarmed to find them,
Who offer, worship, and eat
Day after day.

Goggeshvara,
Your protégés went away,
Leaving the Linga behind.

(VAV 176)

9.

What's known as worldly
Is fake,

What's known as devotion,
A sermon.

What's known as character
Is a fancy,

What's known as likeness,
Pollution.

Not in these four,
Goggeshvara—

Your protégé
Is boundless indeed.

(VAV 524)

10.

When the trace of the body
Is known in the Linga,
The protégé has no qualms of the body,
Look!

When the trace of breath
Is known in knowledge,
There's no fear of clamours,
Look.

The protégé is still,
When he moves,
Silent,
When he speaks.

Listen, Sister dear,
The protégés of Goggeshvara
Have no sign.

(VAV 1277)

11.

Kailasa is a silver hill.
The one that dwells there
    Is a Rudra.

Goggeshvara,
    Your protégés know that
    The hill and the Rudra
    Will be gone in the deluge.

(VAV 1049)

12.

The spoken word
Is the luminous Linga,

Voice,
Is the supreme core of the self.

The palate-lip complex of the protégés
Are beyond sound, speck and trace.

Listen, dear fool,
The protégés of Goggeshvara
Are not polluters
When they speak.

(VAV 1234)

13.

A plant was born
        In the middle of the water.
There came a monkey
        To graze the leaves on the plant.
On the monkey's horns
        Appeared the wonder.

It's impossible to be a protégé
Until the wonder ceases,
        Goggeshvara.

(VAṾ 313)

14.

My Lord,
Is the word of the pious protégé false?

    It's true.
    It's true.

The inner
    Is the world of gods.
The outer
    Is the human world.

When we're beyond these two worlds,
    Let them remain there,
    Goggeshvara!

(VAV 1090)

15.

Four Armed, I say,
When there're two eyes.
Maheshvara, I say,
When there're three eyes.
Sadashiva, I say,
When the body is all eyes.

Goggeshvara,
The matchlessly great Allayya, I say,
When eyes appear on the sole
Of your protégés.

(VAV 1281)

16.

Why a hospice, My Lord?
Why a mountain?
Why people?
Why the absence of people, My Lord,
    For the protégé that has peace in his mind?

Again,
Why thoughts from without,
Meditation,
Silence,
Chanting,
And penance,
    For the protégé that has known the self,
    Goggeshvara, My Lord?

(VAV 1257)

17.

Word we can offer / The feet we can offer,*
        Not the meaning of the word / Not the object.**
Food we can offer,
        Not the offering.

Goggeshvara,
        Your protégés look at what's behind
        And offer what's ahead.

(VAV 172)

---

*The word pada means both 'word' and 'feet'.

**The word padartha means both 'meaning of the word' and 'object'.

18.

Channa Basavanna is my body,
    My Lord.
Madivalayya is my mind,
    My Lord.
Sangana Basavanna is my breath,
    My Lord.

Goggeshvara,
    I live like the most blissful,
    With the might
    Of your protégés
    Seen all over me.

(VAV 918)

19.

When I'm visible within me,
        Will you admire within you?

The world wore out
        In suspicion.

Goggeshvara,
        Your protégés are
        Like the image
        The mirror consumed,

        Like the water
        The iron consumed,

        Like the turmeric
        The sun's scorching light consumed.

(VAV 367)

20.

Can fire be frigid?
        Can venom be delicious, tell me?

Tell me, Linga,
        Can the eye be disguised?

Does the invader have kindness in him?

Do the burglars have a heart?

Goggeshvara,
        Your protégés
        Have no trickery,
        As they know the three worlds.

(VAV 134)

THE TEACHER

1.

Look, a child was born
    Between the teacher and the disciple.

How did it become teacher to the teacher?

Sangana Basavanna,
Look, I prevailed,
    As I bowed down to Channabasavanna,
    The protégé of Goggeshvara,
    Who attained
    The Linga of the beginning.

(VAV 774)

2.

Like the vine in search of, winding on to the leg,
Like the fulfillment of a craving desire,
Like the poor man stumbling upon wealth,

I came, desiring on and on,
    And found the form
    Which the acts of the mind won't reach,
    Look!

I found the flow of my knowledge,
    Look!

I found the fulsome light
    Shining bright, ceaselessly,
    Within me and without,
    Look!

Look, Goggeshvara,
    I prevailed when I found my supreme teacher—
    The great wondrous sight on the palmtop
    With the sign wiped out.

(VAV 753)

3.

Is the body merged in the Linga?
        No, hold on!
Is life merged in the Linga?
        No, hold on!

He that knows the space
        Between body and life
        Is merged in the Linga.

Look, Goggeshvara,
        He that transcends the nine doors
        And stands at the tenth door,
        Is Guru indeed.

(VAV 1373)

4.

Look at the weariness of not finding,
When the visible
Isn't held
And the invisible
Chased.

If the Guru's feet is held
When the visible is seen,
The invisible is found,
Goggeshvara.

(VAV 51)

5.

There's the lamp.
        There's the wick, too.
Where's the light
        When it's lit without oil?

There's Guru.
        There's Linga.
Where's devotion
        Unless the student has risen
        To the true learning?

If you don't offer food
        After listening to 'I'm that'
        I cast it away,
        Goggeshvara.

(VAV 78)

6.

The six schools of vision went astray.
Drank liquor,
Consumed meat.

I became a Guru
As the six schools of vision
Went astray,
Look, Goggeshvara.

(VAV 1040)

7.

The camphor in the flame,
The salt in the water,
The disciple in the hands
    Of the sacred guru—

Do the three have
    Dissimilar ways,
    Goggeshvara?

(VAV 62)

INHERING WITHIN

1.

The fire in the tree burning down the tree—
So have I become,
My friend.
The fragrance of the wind from the field
Embracing the nose—
So have I become,
My friend.
A doll of wax taken by fire—
So have I become,
My friend.

I worshipped
The linga called Goggeshvara
And lost my mortal being,
My friend.

(VAV 396)

2.

When the body borne of earth
Is back in the earth,
Look, the legend of the earth
Is Legend indeed.

When the body borne of water
Is back in the water,
Look, the legend of the water
Is Legend indeed.

When the body borne of fire
Is back in the fire,
Look, the legend of the fire
Is Legend indeed.

When the body borne of air
Is back in the air,
Look, the legend of the air
Is Legend indeed.

When the body borne of sky
Is back in the sky,
Look, the legend of the sky
Is Legend indeed.

When the body borne of Goggeshvara-linga
Is back in the linga,
Look, the legend of the linga
Is Legend indeed.

(VAV 392)

3.

Look at the water that remained water,
Unburnt by the fire within!

When I look out for its state,
It's no water!

Who can fathom the ground
Where he stood
Not merging into the clan,
While living in the clan?

Goggeshvara,
Look at your ways,
Refusing to show themselves
Even as they're within and beyond.

(VAV 3)

4.

Gold, we can test,
    But can we test the colour?

Flower, we can wear,
    But can we wear the fragrance?

Acts, we can perform,
    But can we know the thing?

Siddharamayya,
    'Goggeshvara!'
    We can say,
    But the Linga can't be the self.

(VAV 817)

5.

Show me the place,

Where shower is untouched
By the mind,

Where food is untouched
By the body,

Where worship is untouched
By acts of the mind,

Where sight is untouched
By eyelids,

Where Linga is untouched
By air,

Goggeshvara.

(VAV 419)

6.

What do you know of the ways of Yoga,
Where fire is burnt,
Where water is washed,
Where the sky is seized,
By standing on air.

Learn of the Kadali forest*
From within you.
Don't be proud or envious.
Don't grieve.

Behold,
The Linga called Goggeshvara
Isn't a fantasy.

(VAV 229)

---

*Kadali is the word for plantain, and in extention, a plantain grove. In Shaiva literature, it generally alludes to Srisailam, the pilgrimage centre in Andhra on the river Krishna.

7.

When you come running
And sit on the speaking swing,
It swings without touching,
Like the ocean of existence
That has no return.

What's this carnival of melody
From the bumblebee seated on the swan?

Unbroken was the melody,
With him within.

Do those with a body
Know the mouth with which
Goggeshvara dines?

(VAV 241)

8.

A plantain sapling rose
At the bottom of the heart's well.
Look at the serpent
Come to feed on the plantain!

When the plantain grows with pride
And the serpent rises,
It's formless,
Look, Goggeshvara.

(VAV 243)

9.

I saw a flaming linga
        In the shrine of wax.
Now, where has the priest
        Gone to sport?

Where has the Maya,
        Wound and bound
        To the schools of vision
        Of the Northern Land
        Gone?

I saw the fire in the tree
        Consume the tree.
Where has Goggeshvara-linga
        Gone to sport?

(VAV 418)

10.

They look for reflection
In the mirror
And fail to find it.

It shines
In the polar sphere.

Goggeshvara dwells
In those who know this.

(VAV 1135)

11.

The earth and the sky
        Are the womb of a being.

What's mighty there for him
        That doesn't call it mighty?
What's trifling there for him
        That doesn't call it trifling?

If might moves into the mind,
        Is there a match to it,
        Goggeshvara?

(VAV 20)

RELATIONSHIPS

1.

From where is the mango tree?
From where, the cuckoo?
        From where to where is this bond,
        My friend?

The gooseberry,
The salt from the sea,
        From where to where is this bond,
        My friend?

Between Goggeshvara-linga
And me—
        From where to where is this bond,
        My friend?

(VAV 59)

2.

I saw fragrance flee
    When the bumblebee arrived.
    What wonder, tell me!

I saw intellect flee
    When the mind arrived.

Goggeshvara,
    I saw the shrine flee
    When the Lord arrived.

(VAV 429)

3.

Has the bumblebee savoured the fragrance?
        Or the fragrance, the bumblebee?

Has the linga become the breath?
        Or breath, the linga?

Goggeshvara,
Goggeshvara,
        You alone
        Know the difference.

(VAV 679)

4.

From where did the breath appear
    In the bird within the egg?

What do the sterile beings know
    Of the secret of its speech?

What do the beasts in the jungle know
    The hunter behind the bull,
    Goggeshvara?

(VAV 1252)

5.

Does the fire in the stone
        Flare?
Does the tree in the seed
        Speak?
Not one can see,
        Invisible as it is.

Goggeshvara's ways are seen
        Only by them
        That revel in communion.

(VAV 2)

6.

Your ways are

Like the treasure
Shielded under the earth,
Like the lightning
Shielded in the cloud,
Like the mirage
Shielded in the field,
Like the light
Shielded behind the eyes,

Goggeshvara.

(VAV 4)

7.

Is the Linga within or without?
Tell me, if you know.

Is the Linga left or right?
Tell me, if you know.

Is the Linga ahead or behind?
Tell me, if you know.

Is the Linga gross or subtle?
Tell me, if you know.

Tell me, if you know
Goggeshvara-linga,

Is the Linga the breath,
Or breath, the Linga?

(VAV 153)

8.

Water pollutes
    The moonlight hill.
Fire pollutes
    The sunlight hill.
Taste pollutes
    The touchstone hill.

What's the difference in polluting?

Goggeshvara knows
    The difference in consuming
    The cooked water and cooked fire.

(VAV 252)

9.

Don't be like the slime
    On a tortoise's hatchling,
    Sangana Basavanna!

Don't be like the pact
    Between the crow and the cuckoo,
    Sangana Basavanna!

Don't be like the monkey that leaps
    Without missing a branch,
    Sangana Basavanna!

Don't be like the swan
    That takes away the water from milk,
    Sangana Basavanna!

Tell me, Sangana Basavanna,

    Is it possible to seek again
    After being unmindful
    In Goggeshvara-linga?

(VAV 827)

10.

When the mind's pleasure
    Was brought to the eye,
When the eye's pleasure
    Was brought to the mind,
The mind was wary,

    It was wary.

Goggeshvara,
    The vow is shattered
    When the sites
    Are turned upside down.

(VAV 206)

11.

Flame arose
        From the union of the five elements.
Camphor arose
        From the union of the five elements.

Tell me,
What became of the union of the two,
        Goggeshvara—
        Beyond word and mind.

(VAV 614)

12.

Sound, the horse
Has Vishnu for reins,
The moon and the sun
For footrests,
And Brahma
For saddle.

It became formless,
Where it was form,
For the horseman
Called Goggeshvara.

(VAV 259)

13.

Look at the way condition joined with condition,
        Atom joined with sound,
        And trace united with trace.

It was in the Linga, unwinking.*
        I became 'I, the teacher's feet', my friend.

Look at the way the before and the after united
        To form an image,
        And the Linga became the moving.

To the feet of Sangana Basavanna,
Merged spotlessly in Goggesvara,
        I say, 'I bow down! Yes, I do.'

(VAV 855)

---

*Incidentally, the word *animisha*, 'unwinking', occurs as the name of Allama's guru in the hagiographic works beginning with Harihara's *Prabhudevara Ragale* in the late 12th century.

14.

It was diffident at the talk that the breath is Linga.
The mind was diffident.
The body fell, when the breath departed.

It was diffident when the Linga was in splendour,
The mind was diffident.

Goggeshvara is the might
Not within me.

(VAV 236)

15.

What do you know of the self?
        What'll you see after you are dead?

Today! It's today!
        It's today, O Man!

The troubles of serving Shiva
        Are not like words, look, brothers dear.

It's not dirty words,
Not street talk,
It's the seed of a single night, look!

The union with Goggeshvara is a bond
        Joyful today,
        Virtuous in times ahead.

(VAV 500)

16.

The head is the breast
For a cow without breasts.

Suckle in the mind,
My dear.
Suckle in the mind.

If you can suckle milk after dying,
You're the Linga
Called Goggeshvara,
My dear.

(VAV 248)

17.

What if naked,
        With ash smeared,
        Will he be trailing brahma's path*?

What if sorrow is forgotten
        After gobbling food,
        Will he be trailing brahma's path?

Look, Goggeshvara,
It's effortless release,
        When acts of the mind are bare
        And the mind unclothed.

(VAV 530)

*'Trailing brahma's path' is a means of liberation, but the expression in Kannada, 'brahmachari', also means a celibate student.

18.

Sound is polluted, they say.
    Does sound have pollution
    Beyond one's suspicion?

Does dust ever stick to the wind?

Goggeshvara-linga
    Isn't of this trait,
    O Sangana Basavanna.

(VAV 1018)

19.

On the day
    When the beginning and the end
    Unite,
On the day
    When the moon and the sun
    Unite,
On the day
    When the earth and the sky
    Unite,
Goggeshvara-linga
    Is formless.

(VAV 309)

20.

The body is an island;
        The mind, an island;
Joy, an island;
        The word, an island.

Goggeshvara,
        You dwell there,
        Where the space between
        The four islands
        Are fused together.

(VAV 594)

THE SELF

1.

After witnessing the abode
Of those that vanish,
Survive,
And whirl,

I craved for a self
That has no touch,
Knot,
And form.

I was walking with no feet.
I was gazing with no eyes,
Goggeshvara.

(VAV 745)

2.

The self,
When it walks,
Should walk the wayward walk.
The self,
When it talks,
Should talk the wayward talk.

Should make love
Without a form.
Should make devotion
Without the world.

Goggeshvara,
The self remains
Without knowing who it is.

(VAV 448)

3.

A little bumblebee
Born in the heart's lotus
Flew away to devour the sky,
My friend.

The three worlds
Turned upside-down
In the wind, blowing
From the wings of the bumblebee.

When the five-coloured swan's
Cage was smashed,
The bumblebee fell on the ground,
Its wings broken.

Goggeshvara,
Living in your protégés' communion,
I saw the marvellous secret
Of the rising self.

(VAV 95)

4.

I didn't chase to hold.
I didn't hold to return.

What shall I say?
O Linga,
How shall I say?

After knowing the self,
I wasn't born again,
Look, Goggeshvara.

(VAV 685)

5.

This world and the next dwell
        In the dwelling of the self.
The sky, Meru, and Mandhara dwell
        In the dwelling of the self.
All worlds dwell
        In the dwelling of the self.
The true, the eternal, and the blissful form of Shiva dwells
        In the dwelling of the self.
Beyond the north and the four quarters dwell
        In the dwelling of the self.
The sun, the moon, and the firmament of stars dwell
        In the dwelling of the self.
The distance and the great distance dwell
        In the dwelling of the self.
Goggeshvara-linga, with its own ways, dwells
        In the dwelling of the self.

(VAV 370)

6.

Whom to remember,
  Master,
  After mind has become Linga?

Whom to desire,
  Master,
  After feeling has itself become the union?

Whom to know,
  Goggeshvara,
  After illusion is erased,
  And the self turns real?

(VAV 421)

7.

Look!
A sea of sorrow
    For as little joy as a mustard.

Look at the brag
    Of mating for a moment!

When the self is given away
    For gaining wealth,
    Awareness is lost,
    Goggeshvara!

(VAV 123)

8.

Look, it's ignorance to say,
    'I don't know the self.'

Look, ignoring the ignorance of not knowing,
    It's an inverse feeling to say,
    'I see no knowledge'.

Nowhere can the might
    That shows everything be seen.
The self that can't be seen
    Cannot be shown.
Can the self that can't be shown
    Be known?

Siddharamayya,
Until there's desire for Goggeshvara-linga,
    Know yourself by yourself
    With the anxiety that
    It's not known.

(VAV 1070)

9.

How does it matter
        What you've seen,
        My friend?
He that hasn't seen the self is blind.

How does it matter
        What you've heard,
        My friend?
He that hasn't heard the self is deaf.

How does it matter
        What one has spoken,
        My friend?
He that hasn't spoken the self is dumb.

He must verily see
        His self.
He must verily hear
        His self.
He must verily speak
        His self.

Look, Goggeshvara,
        This, indeed, is the site of the self,
        Its own ground,
        Its own form.

(VAV 1248)

10.

She became a companion to the Linga
When the ways of the body ceased to be.
She became a companion to knowledge
When the ways of the mind ceased to be.
She became a great radiance
When the ways of the acts of the mind ceased to be.

I submit to the stand of Mahadeviyakka
Who turned into a linga herself
In our Goggeshvara-linga,
After the self-other dualism
Was wiped out.

(VAV 1303)

11.

What's called I
  Is the testimony.
What's called you
  Is the testimony.

What's called the self
  Is the testimony.
What's called the other
  Is the testimony.

What's called the testimony
  Is the testimony.
What's called the non-testimony
  Is the testimony.

What's called Goggeshvara
  Is the non-testimony.

(VAV 1408)

12.

The enchanted ones
With impotence lost—

Do they look
For movement in them?
Do they look
For intellect in them?

Merged in the Linga,
Their bodies lost—

Do they look
For movement in them?
Do they look
For intellect in them?

The self, called Goggeshvara,
Is in the ones that remain.

(VAV 684)

THE BODY

1.

The legs are wheels,
Look, My Lord.

The body's a loaded cart,
Look!

Five men drive the cart,
Each unlike the other.

When it's driven
Without knowing its mind,
Its axle breaks,
Goggeshvara.

(VAV 42)

2.

The legs became the pillar,
    My Lord,
    My body turned into a shrine.

My tongue, the bell,
    My head, the golden pinnacle,
    What's up, My Lord?

My breath was the Linga's throne,
    My Lord.

Goggeshvara,
    I stayed in a way
    That didn't topple
    Your Pranalinga,
    Installed in me.

(VAV 195)

3.

Why another shrine
    When there's one in the body?

No one asked for two,
    My Lord.

Goggeshvara,
    What am I,
    When you're a stone?

(VAV 213)

4.

This's a surprise to me,
        Tell me, Sister dear.

Joy without a body,
Existence without life—

Tell Goggeshvara-linga
        Where this abode is.

(VAV 1195)

5.

When the body is without
And the offering within,
Isn't your mind wary of the mind,
My Lord?

Goggeshvara,
The vow is broken
When the offering is found
In Pranalinga.

(VAV 253)

6.

To say, 'I've known',
While wandering with a body
Is a lie indeed.

Sangana Basavanna,
Goggeshvara-linga must be known
Without a stain,
Like dewdrop on a lotus leaf.

(VAV 950)

7.

There's a great Linga on the body,
    But when the Linga in the hand tumbles,
    They bury the body
    Into the earth.

Ah!
    They're shattered—
    The frigid ones that do not know
    Goggeshvara-linga.

(VAV 1013)

8.

He, the blind,
Found a pearl
On the earth-less field.
He, without a hand,
Put it into a string.
He, without a neck,
Wore it.

Is make-up without a body
Thrown into disarray,
Goggeshvara?

(VAV 443)

9.

Without body,
I stood
As I looked on and on.

Without alarm,
I was alarmed
As I looked on and on.

Without form,
I looked,
And found the Linga
Called Goggeshvara.

(VAV 687)

10.

What's it
When you descend
After worship?

What's it
When the impending worship
Is accomplished?

The body is the platform,
Life, the Linga,
Goggeshvara.

(VAV 184)

11.

The body
Is the Pranalinga's platform.

The heavenly Ganga
Is the shower.

Fragrance without flower
Is worship.

The sound, 'Shiva! Shiva!'
In the lotus of the heart.

Look,
This is the non-dual
Goggeshvara!

(VAV 198)

12.

Linga in the body's fist,
The world in the mind's fist,

How'll I call you Pranalinga,
My Lord?

Outwards, it shows as a sign.

The body doesn't find the body,
The mind doesn't find the mind.

How'll I call you Pranalinga,
Goggeshvara?

(VAV 1140)

13.

The pleasure made in the body
Is the Linga's adornment.

It's like wildfire cutting grass.
    No stack behind,
    No grass ahead.

It's fruitful,
    Until the body is Linga.

Merging in the Linga
    Is something else,
    Goggeshvara.

(VAV 204)

14.

Not a matter of training,
Not the pleasure of listening,
Not a matter of sciences
Or communion,
Not a matter of
Within or without.

What's the use of communing
Without knowing its body?

Look, Siddharamayya,
Goggeshvara-linga
Is beyond compare.

(VAV 1341)

15.

I made the body a garden,
    The mind a spade,
    And dug out the root of delusion,
    My Lord.

I broke the lump of the world
    To sow the seed of brahma,
    My Lord.

The undivided cosmos
    Is the well,
The wind,
    The pulley.
I drew water
    From the sushumna nerve,*
Fixed a fence
    Of fairness and restraint
    For fear that the five bulls
    Will destroy it,
And kept watch at all times
    Over the garden
    To raise the crop,
    Look, Goggeshvara.

(VAV 1177)

---

*The sushumna is believed to be the most important nerve in the body, connecting the muladhara to the sahasrara chakra.

16.

There's no bond with others, My Lord,
        There being no body.
Nothing else was explained, My Lord,
        There being no bond with others.
It was freed of bonds, My Lord,
        Nothing else being explained.

Goggeshvara,
        This's how your name is, My Lord.

(VAV 303)

THE WORD

1.

A part was ruined by birth,
        A part, without birth,
A part, ruined by touch,
        A part, without touch.

What's this?
How's this?
        It's impossible to know.

My Lord,
Look at the darkness
        Called 'What's this? How's this?'

Between the two set of words,
        'What's this? How's this?'
        Fire took the three worlds,
        Goggeshvara.

(VAV 228)

2.

Can the metal bruise the body
After it melts into a mass?

Sangana Basavanna,
How can those that speak
In the non-duality of words
Know Goggeshvara-linga?

(VAV 1022)

3.

It didn't touch in the three,
        It didn't show in the six,
It wasn't found in the eight,
        It didn't stand in the one.

What do I tell of it?
        How do I describe it?

It didn't decline in the body.
        It didn't remain in the breath.

The Linga called Goggeshvara
        Didn't appear in the word.

(VAV 667)

4.

Does the corpse cry,
  'I'm dead'?
Does the suppressed desire
  Call out?
Can the fermented milk
  Be sweet?

These are words
  Not agreeable to
  Goggeshvara-linga?

(VAV 1403)

5.

Who offered butter
        And gave a name
        To the child called
        Formlessness?

Ho! Ho! Ho!
        Look at the diffidence of the word!

It tortured the communers
        That failed to make sense of
        Goggeshvara.

(VAV 264)

6.

'Composing a vachana'—
　　Look!
　　It's not like the colour of these words.
All those who were praised
　　Were reduced to images.

Look, Siddharamayya,
　　The three worlds know—
　　With Goggeshvara as witness—
　　That the path of the Vedas and the sciences
　　Know no praise.

(VAV 1067)

7.

‘Smaller than a grain
        And greater than the great’,
These words are false!

Is there deluge
        Where the Linga stands?

Goggeshvara is nowhere
        Other than in the devotees’
        Acts of the mind.

(VAV 77)

8.

The sugarcane stick has base and top,
    But does the sugar stick have them?

The touchstone has base and top,
    But does pure gold have a touchstone?

Siddharamayya,
    When there's an end to the ambiguity
    Between 'it exists'
    And 'it doesn't',
    The self is Goggeshvara-linga.

(VAV 820)

9.

In the abode where nothing exists,
The self created
'You' and 'I'.
What if a thousand things are told
Of what 'doesn't exist'
And 'does exist'?

If 'does exist'
Can be made 'doesn't exist',
Isn't 'doesn't exist'
Goggeshvara?

(VAV 732)

GOGGESHVARA AND I

1.

Are you the Lord?
        No. I'm the Lord.
If you're the Lord,
        Why don't you guard me?

I ask if they would,
        And give an ounce of water.
When hungry,
        I give a handful of food.

I'm the Lord,
        Look, Goggeshvara.

(VAV 558)

2.

Why do you doubt
Whether you've had food and worn clothes?
        Does the fire eat?
        Does the earth wear clothes?

When did you eat?
        When did I see?

Don't be afraid of dying
        At the hands of smoke,
        Without food or cloth.

Don't fear, Goggeshvara,
        You've
        Nothing to be ashamed of.

(VAV 569)

3.

Linga on the body,
        Body on the Linga,
        What's this?

Knowledge on the mind,
        A sign on knowledge,
        What's this?

I, where it's you,
        You, where it's I.

        Goggeshvara,
        There's no divide
        Between 'you' and 'I'.

(VAV 310)

4.

The sound or the speck,
        What came before?

The body or the life,
        What came before?

Tell me,
        You that know
        The living body's rightful abode:
        You or I,
        What came before?

Tell me,
You that know,
        Goggeshvara.

(VAV 659)

5.

On the day you arrived,
I came after you.
The doubts of the day
Were torn apart.

You became the devotee,
And I,
The wandering mendicant,

To form the body
Of Goggeshvara-linga.

(VAV 893)

6.

Is the sense
In the legs,
The hands,
The body
And life
The god?

When the self wipes out the 'I',
Goggeshvara-linga is the self.

(VAV 1383)

7.

There's no such thing as 'I' and 'You'.
There's nothing, nothing indeed,
After the self is known.

From where does the no-ness that doesn't exist
Arrive?

Goggeshvara—who forgot the body
After knowing the state of being—
Is the one without acts of the mind.

(VAV 305)

8.

The eye's pollution was torn away
By making love.
The mind's pollution was gone
With the touch.

The feeling of 'I'
United with Goggeshvara-linga.

(VAV 1380)

9.

I wandered the endless country.
I wore the boundless robe.
I held the hunger-less bowl
    And went begging
    For alms of devotion.

Goggeshvara is hungry.

    Get up,
    Feed him,
    Sangana Basavanna!

(VAV 958)

10.

Water, you must be,
        When cinder rains.
Wind, you must be,
        When water turns deluge.
Sky, you must be,
        When it's the great deluge.
Get rid of the self, you must,
        In the cosmic deluge.

The Linga called Goggeshvara
        You must be.

(VAV 556)

11.

The poets of old
Are my concubine's children.
The poets to come
Are my compassion's kids.

The poets of the sky
Are infants in my cradle.
Hari and Brahma
Are my affectionate farmhands.

You're the father-in-law,
I, the son-in-law,
Goggeshvara.

(VAV 550)

12.

There was a spec
    In the subtle duct of the firmament,
    Chanting 'I'm that, I'm that.'

In the fulfillment of turning weary
    Of dining on the nectar,
    I had my abode within you,
    Goggeshvara.

(VAV 247)

13.

Annoyance is wrecked.
I know the gift you confer.
I'm not in need of it.

What I ask for
        Isn't in your face,
        Goggeshvara.

(VAV 548)

14.

The divine retainers of heaven
Are without me.
Is it true?

The noble devotees,
Truthful and pious,
Are without me.
Is it true?

Let them dwell
In the fourteen worlds.
I dwell in you,
Goggeshvara.

(VAV 551)

15.

Will I ask for Devendra's seat?

Don't run, like the glow of the rising sun.
    Don't run before me, like the ruby's shine.

Look!
Speak to me!

Goggeshvara,
    Is there in me
    The Linga that begs deceitfully?

(VAV 988)

16.

Do not shoot, Kama,
    Do not shoot.

Your shaft is false, Ho!

Lust, anger, desire,
Delusion, pride, envy—
    Are these not enough for you?

Scorched in separation from Goggeshvara-linga,
    Can they be scorched again,
    You silly Kama?

(VAV 147)

17.

Look, my friend,
I arrived in the company of the five.
Look, my friend,
I stood in the company of the five.

The five moved on
Along their own paths.

Ah!
I alone remained,
With no companions.

I saw the formless might
Called Goggeshvara,
Forever blissful.

(VAV 397)

GOD IS DEAD, THERE'S NO GOD

1.

There was an elephant
        In the rice.

The rice was scorched,
        The elephant survived.

What wonder is this,
        My Lord?

The God perished,
        The Goddess went whoring,
        I prevailed,
        Goggeshvara.

(VAV 454)

2.

The horns of Aja—
    The creator of the world—
    Broke.
The sun and the moon on earth
    Fell on the ground.

It's sunset
    When the sunrise has stopped.
The village was scorched,
    The sound ended.

    What wonder is this?

The God perished,
    The Goddess went whoring,
    I prevailed,
    Goggeshvara.

(VAV 539)

3.

Ah, the elders,
Great and matching warriors of renown,
Have lost their mind
And driven mad!

The God perished,
Brahma carried,
Vishnu held the fire.
Ganga and Gauri
Became tonsured widows.

I saw this in alarm,
Goggeshvara.

(VAV 549)

4.

Goddess Ganga
Became a tonsured widow.

Goddess Gauri
Lost her earrings.

The moon and the sun
Bathed for pollution.

The Wind God
Bore the carriage heavenward-bound.

Vasudeva
Ripped the skull apart.

News from there:
Goggeshvara is dead!

(VAV 1210)

5.

Don't befriend the thief
Who transcended
The life in the body.

Take care of your belongings.

Not one is there to weep
When the thief called Goggeshvara
Is killed.

(VAV 140)

6.

What if they eat?
What if you don't?
What's touched,
And what untouched?
It doesn't match,
For it isn't born.

Goggeshvara died,
Prevailed,
And remained carefree.

(VAV 575)

7.

Given as he is to desire and dreams,
He that's called Brahma
Fails the vow.

He that's called Vishnu
Fell dead.

He that's called Rudra
Is an unrestrained fool.

The mindless murder that took everyone
Will reach you,
Goggeshvara.

(VAV 508)

8.

If I'm the devotee
        And you the Lord,
Do they blend
        The common sap?
Do they blend
        The earth and the sky,
And play percussion
        With the moon and the sun?

Listen,
        You're Ganga in the matted hair.
Listen,
        You're Gauri on the lap.

When Goggeshvara-linga
        Perishes at my hands,
        Is it proper for you
        To gobble the whore's food?

(VAV 234)

9.

Not on the earth,
        Not in the sky,
Not within or without
        The fourteen worlds.

They don't know what,
        They don't know how,
Tell me, ye.

Let's not speak
        Of the ages past.

Neither did Goggeshvara exist then,
        Nor does he exist now.

(VAV 650)

10.

They hold food
For the love of hunger.
They've a shower
For the love of thirst.

There's no Lord,
No devotees.
I don't exist.
Neither do you.

Goggeshvara,
There're no worshippers,
Nor the worshipped.

(VAV 626)

11.

Not on earth,
Not in the sky.
    Neither in the fourteen world of worlds,
    Nor yonder.

I don't know what happened,
    My dear.

Goggeshvara wasn't then,
    Isn't now,
    And never will be.

(VAV 621)

SPECTRES OF RUIN

1.

Look, a wild serpent arrived
And sunk its fangs,
When I went to live in a house
Built in a ruined village!

Mad elephants
That revealed the fierce goddess
Were roving street after street!

When the papers with Chitragupta
Were made sense of,
The ruined village was ruined,
Goggeshvara.

(VAV 328)

2.

The ogress's daughter who held in check
        The rock on the sea
        And the lightning that struck the well,
        Perished in the jungle.

The script that can't be erased
        Cannot be written,
        Look!

The mid-water glow
        Is on the edge of the wind,
        Look!

When the self with no beginning,
And the middle with no end
Are seized in the deserted village,

        The fierce goddess devoured them,
        Goggeshvara.

(VAV 678)

3.

I've become the impossible.
I know the ways of the world,
        For I've seen them.

The world will not remain,
        My Lord.

Don't ruin
        By doing on and on!
Don't turn insane
        For the country!

Goggeshvara,
        Beg me for formlessness.

(VAV 536)

4.

The fire in the village
Burnt in the jungle.
The fire in the jungle came
To take the village.

Listen, ho!
Listen to the heat
In the four quarters.

When the eyes met the raging sound,
A thousand torsos shook,
And died countless deaths,
Goggeshvara.

(VAV 536)

5.

A forest was born
        In the sky.
There lives a hunter
        In the forest.
The hunter captured a deer.

The hunter can't perish
        Without killing the deer.

Does awareness come from a naught,
        Goggeshvara?

(VAV 319)

6.

Ah!
When a house was built
        In the deserted forest,
        A wildfire arose to take it.

Where has the landlord gone,
        When the house is on fire
        In the village?

The landlord weeps and grieves
        When the house burnt in the village
        Isn't destroyed.

Looking at the abode that has no love for you,
        I left in disgust,
        Goggeshvara.

(VAV 76)

7.

When it rained
On the Northern Land,
Drought befell the country.

All creatures in the country
Perished.

I look for you, Goggeshvara,
In the burning ground
Where they were consigned to the flames.

(VAV 227)

8.

The night is a face,
    The day, a face,
The body, a face,
    Life, a face.

It doesn't know the intellect,
    Look!
The madness called Pranalinga,
    Look!

Thus,
    Goggeshvara,
    Have the three worlds perished.

(VAV 496)

9.

Sanaka, Sanandana,*
And all the sages,
All those with ash smeared
On their bodies—

It's a lie
That they're true,
It's a lie
That they're eternal.

They perished,
That's the truth,
Goggeshvara!

(VAV 505)

*The four Kumaras, Sanaka, Sanandana, Sanatana and Sanatkumara, are identified in Pauranic legends as celibate sages born of Brahma's mind.

10.

Five corpses fell
        In the middle of the village
        In the forest
        Of the eye.

They arrive
        And weep on and on,
        As there're great many relatives.

The corpse doesn't bake,
        The forest doesn't douse.

The carriage to heaven
        Is up in flames,
        Goggeshvara.

(VAV 26)

11.

Look how the elders on earth
Withered away
Placing the corpse called costume
On the lance called desire!

Goggeshvara,
I was abashed
To find the elders
Whirling around
With desire before them.

(VAV 466)

12.

Whirling on and on
For the body's flaws,
Reminiscing on and on
For flaws of the mind,
Knowing on and on
For flaws of the acts of the mind,
Speaking on and on
For flaws of the sound,
The Linga called Goggeshvara
Failing to be in the mind…

(VAV 526)

13.

Nobody knew that
He was there,
        As body to the body
        As mind to the mind
        As life to life.

They went astray, saying,
        'It's far,
        It's near,
        Goggeshvara, the Master,
        Is within,
        Is without.'

(VAV 155)

14.

Seven breasts, eight faces, fourteen mouths,
    And a hundred and twenty sharp tusks
    In the twenty-five heads!

Fondling the fire hidden in the heart,
Devouring the purpose of sound,
The colours of the mind subsided,

    The mother that brought forth
    Devoured the son,

    The child gave birth to the mother,

    And the breast on the palmtop
    Devoured the abode
    Called Goggeshvara.

(VAV 17)

15.

I saw the fire born of water,
        Sweltering it.

I saw a mango tree
        In the sky.

I saw a wingless bird
        Devour the field,
        Goggeshvara.

(VAV 292)

16.

The reticence behind shyness
    Went hiding under the yarn.

And there, the erudite seniors—
    Proud of their learning—
    Lost their mind.

When the yarn was sold
    To buy cotton,
    It was gone,
    Goggeshvara.

(VAV 330)

17.

I saw a swan build a nest
    On a peepal tree.

An infant girl
    Was swinging
    On a swing in the nest.

Look, Goggeshvara,
    Pranalinga is seen
    When the swing breaks
    And the girl falls dead on the ground.

(VAV 208)

18.

He is a learned jailor
Who broke the water's limbs,
Cut off the fire's ears and nose,
Beheaded the air,
        And took the sky
        With a lance.

He is a learned jailor
        Who baffled the king,
        The commander,
        And the minister.

Goggeshvara shut the door of nine gates,
        Fastened it with locks,
        And killed nine thousand people,
        So he could prevail.

(VAV 541)

19.

Ah, the monkey that came
    Hopping around
    Devoured the chanting saint!

'Don't! Don't!'
    Said a hare
    From the street in front.

Goggeshvara,
    The blanket devoured
    The hare ahead
    And the monkey behind.

(VAV 543)

20.

The red in the battle's eye,
The red in the battle's mind,
        Whom will it not hound, my friend?

The speck has stuck in the lotus
        And remains there,
        Look!

I was saying, 'There's no Linga,'
        After devouring the blessing
        Called Goggeshvara.

(VAV 611)

DARKNESS AND LIGHT

1.

If the limited light is placed
In the unlimited darkness,
        Light and darkness are both alike.

What wonder is this?
        One isn't afraid of the other!

I was alarmed to see
        The elephant and the lion
        Dining together,
        Goggeshvara.

(VAV 499)

2.

Look at the light,
Look at the darkness
When it's still there!

Look at the wealth,
Look at the poverty
When it's still there!

Look at the offering,
Look at the deluge
When it's received!

Look at Goggeshvara!
Look at this madness!

(VAV 462)

3.

Is it sunrise?
Sunset gone?
O, they've all gone,
        Forms made of formlessness.*

Darkness caved in
        Over the three worlds.

Tell me,
What wonder is this,
        Goggeshvara?

(VAV 41)

*The word *niraalada*, 'of formlessness', is replaced in most versions by *neeralaada*, 'of water'.

4.

Darkness
On the hands that grab,
My friend.
Darkness
In the eye that sees,
My friend.
Darkness
In the mind that recalls,
My friend.

Darkness
All over here,
My friend.
Goggeshvara
Is on the other side,
My friend.

(VAV 219)

5.

I saw a dead hen
Rise and cluck.
I saw the final mango tree
Speak.

I saw darkness
Turn into light.
I saw waking up early
To lose the way.

I don't know what's up,
Goggeshvara.

(VAV 439)

6.

What shall I say
    Of the glory of the mason
    That builds the tank?

Look at the fatigue
    Of digging up the earth
    To draw water!

What ignorance is this
    To break a stone
    And offer food to another stone?

Goggeshvara,
    I was alarmed
    By the ways of this darkness.

(VAV 1058)

7.

Stepping back to see your light,
It was like the rise of
A hundred million suns,
My Lord!

I was wonderstruck
To watch the secret
Of the lightning vine.

Goggeshvara,
If you're the luminous Linga,
Not one can find a simile,
My Lord!

(VAV 1179)

8.

When the light in the light was churned,
It dissolved again.

Look at the devotees
That made a feast of Meru!

I saw the virgin devour the Linga
That fed on meat,
Goggeshvara.

(VAV 1369)

9.

Some say
    They've found.
Some say
    They haven't.

Is it the sidereal sphere?
    Is it the solar sphere?

Goggeshvara dwells
    In the Moon Hill city.

(VAV 1126)

10.

There was a wax pillar
        On the cinder hill,
        Look, Master.

There was a swan
        On the wax pillar.

The pillar burnt.

The swan flew away,
        Goggeshvara.

(VAV 605)

THE ANTI-CAUSAL UNIVERSE

1.

A plant grew
    With no water, shade, or roots.
A deer with no head
    Came to feed on the plant.
A blind man, with no eyes,
    Found the deer.
A hunter with no hands
    Shot the deer.

Goggeshvara,
    When it was taken
    To the country with no fire
    And baked for food,
    It was offering for the Linga.

(VAV 561)

2.

The ogress bore two children,
        Five in the cradle.
What becomes of the children
        When the ogress delivers a child!

I'll rock the cradle.
I'll sing the lullaby.

The cradle devoured the ogress.

Tell me, what's this,
        Goggeshvara.

(VAV 14)

3.

I saw a headless head
Devour the sphere of the earth,
Five hundred million in extent.

I looked at it in alarm
Without a head.

When the sphere of nine divisions emerged,*
Was there anyone
That saw the head,
Goggeshvara?

(VAV 29)

*The earth, it is believed, is made of nine divisions or continents around an axis called Mount Meru.

4.

A new bird was born
In the sky.
It built a nest
With its own joy.

The one bird turned
Into twenty-five.

Brahma became
The bird's cage;
Vishnu,
Food for the bird to peck;
Rudra,
The bird's captive.

The form and the name were lost
When the child in front of the three
Was devoured.

How's this,
Goggeshvara?

(VAV 15)

5.

Ah!
When a termite took the cloth,
The star was feeding
On the sky.

It devoured the darkness
And also the light.

The dead carried the living,
Goggeshvara!

(VAV 602)

6.

Ah!
The coconut sapling
    On the palmtop
    Devoured the stain in the sky.

Ah!
The atom of ruby
    In the pillar
    Devoured the nine million Brahmas.

Ah!
The egg born of egg
    Devoured several birds
    To become formless,
    Goggeshvara!

(VAV 671)

7.

Look, the cow in the chamber
Of the master of the three worlds
        Yields milk
        To none but the one
        That can yoke the wind's noose
        To the sky,
        To milk after killing the cow,
        And breaking the pot.

The milch is the barren,
        The barren, the milch.
        Goggeshvara is the formless
        Without a double.

(VAV 245)

8.

The man with the headless head
Has a heartless body,
Look!

The lover has for a wife
A woman with no body.

In their womb
My mother was born!

I was born,
Married mother,
Made love to her,
And remained faultless,
Look, Goggeshvara.

(VAV 9)

9.

A shrine beyond the city,
A mendicant woman in the shrine,
    Look, Master.

A needle in the woman's hand.

On its edge,
    The fourteen worlds.

Goggeshvara,
    I saw an ant devour
    The woman,
    The needle,
    And the fourteen worlds.

(VAV 431)

10.

The wife was born
        Before the husband
        And remained younger to him.

When the husband made love to her
        After learning that
        She was a sibling,
        A child was born of them!

When the mother fondled the baby,
        It hugged the mother.
        Tell me,
        What's this?

Goggeshvara-linga's devotion
        Was transformed
        When it saw the mother rise
        To offer devotion
        To the husband.

(VAV 80)

11.

I saw the hand bring forth,
When the mind was with child.
I saw the ear drink
The camphor's whiff.
I saw the nose swallow
The radiance of the pearl.
I saw the hungry eyes
Swallow the diamond.

Goggeshvara,
I saw the three worlds
Contained in a sapphire.

(VAV 101)

12.

When a frog devoured the sky,
Rahu caught up with it
Right away!

Look at the strange wonder
Of the blind man
Catching a snake!

For this reason,
I came to learn
Without getting lost in the world,
Goggeshvara.

(VAV 277)

13.

The milk in the lion's mouth,
The butter in the fire's hands,
And the child on the hilltop
Are flowing.

Call him, ho!
To drink the milk.

Behold him
That leaves on the elephant
Of the master of the gods,

Call him, ho!

Goggeshvara,
What shall I say
Of the fingers chopped off,
Lacing on the head
On Hara's churning lance?

(VAV 238)

14.

A little hill appeared
    On a flower;
Six hills appeared
    On a cat.

Those on the hill
    Looked for the stone;
    None found them.

A hill
With ten million and nine hundred thousand faces…

    I'm in one of them,
    Look, Goggeshvara.

(VAV 767)

15.

A bumblebee blossomed on the plant
At the same time as the plant arose.

Look at the bumblebee!

Look at the bumblebee
With your soul full!

Look at the bumblebee
With the supreme soul full!

It fell at Goggeshvara-linga's feet
In great wonder.

Look at the bumblebee!

(VAV 306)

16.

Ah, there was a well
On the palm treetop!
Ah, a hare arrived
To feed on the grass
At the bottom of the well!

I swear on you,
Goggeshvara,
They don't know
How to cook life
Together with the body.

(VAV 286)

PASSIONS OF THE VOID

1.

The sky sang a lullaby
When the wind fell asleep.

Formlessness offered breasts
When the void was tired.

The sky was quite.
The lullaby ended.

Goggeshvara exists,
As if he doesn't.

(VAV 668)

2.

The void sowed the void,
    The void raised the void,
    The void turned into void
    To become the void.

The void's life is void,
    The acts of the void's mind, void,
    The void turned into void
    To become the void.

They that worshipped you
    Became the void long ago.

I worshipped you
    To become the void,
    Goggeshvara.

(VAV 639)

3.

In the times when there was no
        Beginning and base,
The times when there was no
        Pride and bias,
Times when there was no
        Form and formlessness,
When there was no
        Void and non-void,
When the moving and the static
        Weren't made yet,

Goggeshvara,
        That was when
        Your protégé arose.

(VAV 5)

4.

That I've known
Is void indeed.
That I haven't
Is void indeed.

Goggeshvara is void indeed
In knowing,
Sign,
And forgetting.

(VAV 623)

5.

The body without a head
Devoured the world.
The head without a body
Devoured the sky.

The mind strayed
When the body and the head
Were apart.

When the void devoured
The body and the head,
I devoured
Without Goggeshvara.

(VAV 400)

6.

Brahma appeared in adhara.
Vishnu, in svadhisthana.
Rudra, in manipuraka.
Ishvara, in anahata.
Sadashiva, in vishuddhi.
The one beyond compare, in ajna.*

Goggeshvara, I saw them all
    Born in the void,
    Raised in the void,
    Wearing the void as Linga,
    Depend on the void,
    And become the void.

(VAV 201)

---

*Adhara or muladhara, svadhisthana, manipuraka, anahata, vishuddhi and ajna are the six chakras visualized along the spinal column. The kundalini, coiled like a serpent and lying dormant in the muladhara at the base of the spinal column, is believed to rise through these chakras, to reach the seventh chakra, the sahasrara, which is imagined to be on the crown of the head.

7.

When life departs
    In fear of the body's angst,
    Existence doesn't cease,
    Nature doesn't go away.

When it's all about void,
    They say they've perished
    And merged in God.

I'm aghast
    At this talk of void.

If the deathless death is known
    When the body remains,
    It's nothing else
    But Goggeshvara.

(VAV 1051)

8.

They yoke it to the hand.
        They yoke it to the throat.
They yoke it to the body.
        They yoke it to the head.

Not one yokes the Linga
        To the mind.

They die for the void,
        For the forebears are gone.

        Is dying seemly,
        Goggeshvara?

(VAV 1010)

9.

There's neither truth,
        Nor untruth.
Neither born together,
        Nor not born together.

Neither I,
        Nor you.
Neither 'Neither'!
        Nor 'Nor'!

What's called Goggeshvara
        Is a void indeed.

(VAV 1362)

10.

The rising speck
Turned into the form.
The middle speck
Turned into the un-form.
The upper speck
Turned into the non-void.

They merged in the three-fold Linga
To become the void in
Goggeshvara-linga.

(VAV 1384)

11.

The dirt in the eye,
The thorn in the feet,
And the suspicion in the mind,

Were torn apart,
When the act of the mind
Called Goggeshvara
Turned into a void.

(VAV 1381)

12.

The seed of the sky
        Was made of fire.
It sprouted and grew
        With no branches.
It destroyed him that said
        He knew.

O Man, unaware of this judgement,

        Goggeshvara is
        The passion of the void.

(VAV 590)

13.

In the void where nothing exists,
There arose a colour
Born of thought.

The void assumed a form
When it embellished the colour.

Isn't the beauty of such a form
The first frame of
Our Goggeshvara-linga?

(VAV 699)

14.

A god in the village,
        A god in the lake,
A god in the jungle,
        A god on the lap.

Water joined the water,
        The void joined the void,
        The god called man is formless!

What's called Linga
        Is the endless' name.
What's this
        That's called Goggeshvara?

(VAV 525)

15.

As long as the body remains,
It's impossible to be
Without shadow,

As long as the earth remains,
It's impossible to be
Without the sky,

As long as I remain,
It's impossible to be
Without you.

As Goggeshvara-linga
Is under Shakti's spell,
There's no simile
To the utter void.

(VAV 705)

16.

Nowhere else,
But within the self,
        Is the abode of the rift-less,
        Not yoked on
        To rift after rift.

The elders of the void
        Seek for the void.

Tell me, if it's there,
        Goggeshvara?

(VAV 256)

17.

The surroundings were invisible,
There came the raid from the void, Ho!

The darkness of mist,
    Unfathomable,
    Engulfed the sphere of the shafts.

The axle of the sun's chariot
    Broke away.

Goggeshvara,
    The elders lost their way
    When they found Rahu
    Taking the place of the lunar line.

(VAV 504)

18.

The crop without the earth is
The royal meal,
The nameless food.

The cow, untouched by the bull—

I found the butter, and ate it up,
When there was none to churn.

Goggeshvara is the nameless void,
Like an infant's dream.

(VAV 661)

19.

Brahma subsumed the gross body.
Vishnu subsumed the subtle body.
Rudra subsumed the causal body.
Ishvara subsumed the non-body.
Sadashiva subsumed the blissful.
The one beyond the skies
        Subsumed the formless.

Those from the six places
Subsumed the void
And turned into the void,
        Look, Goggeshvara.

(VAV 620)

First-line Index

ALSO IN SPEAKING TIGER CLASSICS

THE ANT WHO SWALLOWED THE SUN

The Abhangs of the Marathi Women Saints

Translated by Neela Bhagwat and Jerry Pinto

One colour now, one colour, You and me, one colour.
I look at You, Panduranga, one look, no You, no me.

The Bhakti movement, which began around the 6th century, transformed Indian thought in fundamental ways. It took seed in Maharashtra in the early 13th century in the form of the Warkari movement. With unmatched passion and eloquence, the Warkari saint-poets spread the message of universal humanism combining it with a deep devotion towards Vitthal. *The Ant Who Swallowed the Sun* is a collection of translations of abhangs by prominent and lesser-known Marathi women-saints belonging to this movement.

These women came from diverse backgrounds: Muktabai was Saint Dynaneshwar's sister; Janabai was a maid in Saint Namdev's household, Rajai his wife and Gonai his mother; Bahinabai, a Brahmin trapped in a difficult marriage; Kanhopatra, a sex-worker; Soyarabai and Nirmala were from lower castes; and not much is known about Bhagu and Vatsara. At a time when women hardly had any autonomy, each claimed Vitthal as their own, addressing him variously as the divine, the lover or the friend. Their abhangs are not just expressions of devotion but offer a scathing criticism of patriarchy and caste hierarchies. With Neela Bhagwat and Jerry Pinto's pitch-perfect translations, *The Ant Who Swallowed the Sun* is an important addition to Bhakti literature, as well as a delight for poetry lovers.